T0130274

Colors For Life

A WORKBOOK

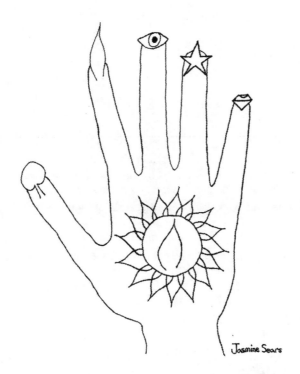

Jasmine Sears

MARTHA SORIA SEARS

BALBOA
PRESS

A DIVISION OF HAY HOUSE

Copyright © 2012 Martha Soria Sears

All rights reserved. No part of this book may be used or reproduced by any means, graphic, electronic, or mechanical, including photocopying, recording, taping or by any information storage retrieval system without the written permission of the publisher except in the case of brief quotations embodied in critical articles and reviews.

Balboa Press books may be ordered through booksellers or by contacting:

Balboa Press
A Division of Hay House
1663 Liberty Drive
Bloomington, IN 47403
www.balboapress.com
1-(877) 407-4847

Because of the dynamic nature of the Internet, any web addresses or links contained in this book may have changed since publication and may no longer be valid. The views expressed in this work are solely those of the author and do not necessarily reflect the views of the publisher, and the publisher hereby disclaims any responsibility for them.

The author of this book does not dispense medical advice or prescribe the use of any technique as a form of treatment for physical, emotional, or medical problems without the advice of a physician, either directly or indirectly. The intent of the author is only to offer information of a general nature to help you in your quest for emotional and spiritual well-being. In the event you use any of the information in this book for yourself, which is your constitutional right, the author and the publisher assume no responsibility for your actions.

Any people depicted in stock imagery provided by Thinkstock are models, and such images are being used for illustrative purposes only.

Certain stock imagery © Thinkstock.

ISBN: 978-1-4525-4665-0 (sc)
ISBN: 978-1-4525-4664-3 (e)

Printed in the United States of America

Balboa Press rev. date: 02/15/2012

This book would not have been possible without the loving support and participation of my family. All my love and thanks to my children Jasmine, Castile, and Cheney, my parents Martha & Roberto Soria, and my friend for life Louis Sears.

CONTENTS

PREFACE

What if I was to tell you that coloring pictures is a fun and easy way to solve those problems, situations, fears that have been causing you stress and anxiety?

Martha Soria Sears is a clinical hypnotherapist, and a business and personal transformation consultant. For over thirty years she has given classes and coached people from all walks of life. Martha uses a multi-disciplinary approach that includes working with the five senses, color, visualization, and hypnotherapy. Her unique approach has been proven successful in stress management, problem solving, finding clarity of purpose, and attaining balance and harmony.

The approach taught in this book evolved out of work sessions with clients. Early on in her work, Martha noticed that talking with people and providing information was not enough to bring about change in their situation. Her clients felt they needed to own their solution in a more tangible way. Martha responded to this need by developing tools that allowed her clients to participate in the solution design by allowing their subconscious to provide input and feedback throughout the process.

The original concept was that the inner-self was trying to express an emotion or an element of stress. One vehicle for this expression was color. The exercise was to use crayons to color pictures; selecting at random the color to use. The intent was not to have pretty pictures but rather to kick-start the internal dialogue process. During their sessions, Martha and her clients would together decipher what the subconscious was expressing. Once the expression was understood, they would develop action plans. One action being to re-color the same picture with the intent of having it represent the desired state of mind.

At first, clients would feel self-conscious about producing pictures where the color was scribbled across the boundaries of the design. Others produced pictures with purple trees and people with green skin. After a few work sessions, people began to feel a sense of relief and calmness. Some clients made this exercise a part of their morning routine so that they would arrive at work feeling clear headed and energized. Other clients said they would keep a coloring book and crayons in their desk drawer at work. If they started to feel stressed out they would pull out their coloring book and color for a few minutes. These people found that taking just a couple of minutes to color would clear their heads enough to tackle what was facing them. The most common benefit expressed was that this exercise gave people the ability to diffuse stress and enhance their creative mind.

After many years and hundreds of pictures, some patterns began to emerge. Martha documented these patterns and used them to develop a guide for interpreting the more common applications of color. This allowed her clients to perform their own translations.

SECTION I

Introduction

How to Use this Book

Have you ever observed a young child with their coloring book, using strokes that appear to go in all directions and colors that don't reflect reality? And, did you happen to notice how satisfied maybe even happy they looked when they were finished? Often as children, we inherently know what we need to do to stay healthy and happy. Get ready to discover the quickest, simplest, and most enjoyable way to decipher your internal dialogue and use it to bring about healing, clarity, and peace.

The basic premise used in this exercise is that we are energy and are surrounded by energy. Each frequency at which this energy vibrates correlates to a color. Energy emanates from us and at the same time we are absorbing energy; every situation is an exchange of energy between us and our environment. Some color therapists even go as far as to say that this is why we display angry people with a red head, or sickly people as green. The thought is that these expressions got started because at some level people feel this color vibration emanating from the person. Some studies have been conducted where a group of people with violent tendencies are surrounded by a color to calm them. For example violent criminals being put in a room that is all pink. These studies have shown that the color does in fact have an effect on the person. These same studies show that when the same violent people are removed from the pink room their violent nature slowly returns to its original levels. This tells us two key things: First, that the effect of color is real; second, that in order to sustain the desired effects it takes more than just one application. The reason is that the person's energy needs to be re-programmed until it can sustain itself at the new frequency.

This brings us to how we absorb color. It is a well known fact that our senses are always registering information, even if we are not conscious of it. In recent years the awareness of color has increased from choosing color schemes that look best on us based on our personality type, to using color to improve our moods and health.

A study by the Psychology Department, University of Waikato, Hamilton, New Zealand tested the effects of color on preschool children. The results were positive. The physical strength and the mood of creative production were measured for six preschool children under six colored room conditions in an ABACAB design. Physical strength and high positive mood were demonstrated in a pink-colored room while the reverse was found in a blue-colored room. The results were interpreted as supporting the differential arousal function of colors.

A San Diego State University School of Nursing controlled study in 1982 involved 60 middle-aged women suffering from rheumatoid arthritis. The patients placed their hands into a box with a blue light and were exposed for 15 minutes. This resulted in significant pain relief which improved with further exposure.

Earlier in this chapter we explored the concept that energy is a bi-directional flow. We also talked about how exposing ourselves to a particular color can bring about a change either in our mood or in our physical self. "But, what does this all mean to me?" you might ask. Well let's take a very common problem in our lives today and see how we can apply these concepts to address it.

Stress is a problem that plagues all of us, regardless of race, socio-economic status, age or gender. Prolonged levels of high stress in our lives can take both an emotional and a physical toll. But, stress does not appear without a reason. Stress requires a trigger, a source, a reason to exist. If we take a look at stress from another perspective we can say that stress is our subconscious trying to tell us that something in our existence is not in balance with the rest of us. Stress is telling ourselves that we need to correct something. But, because we are not fluent in the same language as our subconscious, we misinterpret and continue on without fixing what is wrong. And as we continue, through our lack of understanding, to ignore our warning signals we push ourselves and other aspects out of balance into a spiral downward. Does this sound familiar?

Now sometimes a person does realize that stress is a signal of a deeper problem; for example, unhappiness with a job or a relationship. When this happens the person believes that they must make a major change in order to alleviate stress and so they change jobs, or careers, or relationships. For a while they feel relief and to some extent are happy again. In some cases this might be enough. But, in others the stress returns and they begin a pattern of making major changes in an attempt to escape the stress. Well what if what is causing the stress is not the job or relationship – but something deeper, something within the job or relationship? And, what if we could understand the specific aspect that is causing us stress? And, taking it a step further, what if we could find ways to resolve the specific problem with the job or relationship? By catching these problems early on we can heal the situation before it gets to a point where we feel we have to remove ourselves from it. And then, what if the way to address these problem areas only took a couple of minutes of your time and was even fun to do? Would you then be tempted to take charge of your stress? It's not as farfetched as you might think.

This workbook uses coloring exercises to trigger your creative state of mind and help you better understand the language of your internal dialogue. The ensuing dialogue can help you address those problems that are causing stress in your life.

The first part of the exercise is to select the color from your crayon or pencil box that most appeals to you. The assumption here is that this might be the color you are vibrating at or it may be a color that you are lacking. If this is the color you are vibrating at then the color will come about in strong strokes. Depending on how strong your vibrations are, you might feel like taking the strokes beyond the boundaries of the design on the page. What is happening is that you are venting this energy by expressing its representative color. If on the other hand this color asks for soft timid strokes, then what is happening is that your energy is expressing the need to be "fed" this color.

The second part of the exercise is to decipher or translate your picture. The translation guides provide suggested actions on how to respond to what your sub-conscious has expressed. As you will see, once you get into the exercises, the suggested actions go beyond the use of color.

Each of the nine designs included in this book have a symbolism aimed at addressing a specific aspect of life. The title of each design explains the aspect to which it speaks. It is not expected that you color the pages sequentially. Rather, focus on an aspect of your life that you want to explore. Review the titles of the drawings and select the one that is closest to what you want to work on.

A suggestion on how to approach this exercise: don't read ahead to the translation guides. Look at the design for a few moments, then at your colors. In this part of the exercise you are learning to listen to your inner-self. Don't put expectations on what color will emerge, just allow your sight to guide you. Gaze over the various colors and see which one stands out. Or, you might find yourself coming back to a color over and over. Or, a color triggers a reaction in you. All of these indicate that you are reacting to that color, so listen to it without judgment. After you finish your coloring you will have lots of time to analyze what you did. For now, give the exercise a chance to start this dialogue between you and your energies. At some point during your color session you might feel that you don't want to color anymore. Listen to yourself and stop; even if your picture still has blank areas. We are not looking for pretty pictures; this is not an art exercise. We are looking for clues as to the status of your energy.

Once your coloring session is complete, proceed to Section III. Section III provides a translation guide for each diagram. The more you work with these exercises the more you will be tempted to try and translate as you color. Fight this urge because it can interfere with the process; you could end up coloring what you want to show up and block the communications. To avoid this conflict, work to keep your mind blank as you do your coloring. If a blank mind is difficult for you, then think about walking on the beach or anything else that takes your mind away from what you are doing. That being said, I have had people tell me that as they get deep into the coloring sessions they begin to have flash backs of events or thoughts that are specific to the problem at hand. Honor these by making a note about them somewhere on the page you are coloring. Because just like you are trying to learn the language of your subconscious, your subconscious is continually looking for better ways to communicate with you. Sometimes a coloring session creates a bridge that allows the information locked in your subconscious to come spilling forth. This information can be in colors that you actually see in your mind's eye, or symbols, or memories. Treat each one of these as additional information. Write the impressions on the page and then clear your mind again and continue with the coloring. Then after the coloring session is complete use the notes on the page and factor them into the translation.

Welcome to this adventure with colors, and enjoy the journey.

BIBLIOGRAPHY

Hamid PN, Newport AG., "Effect of colour on physical strength and mood in children" Percept Motor Skills (August, 1989) pp. 179-85

SECTION II

Coloring Exercises

Mystic Hand

Balancing Life's Energies

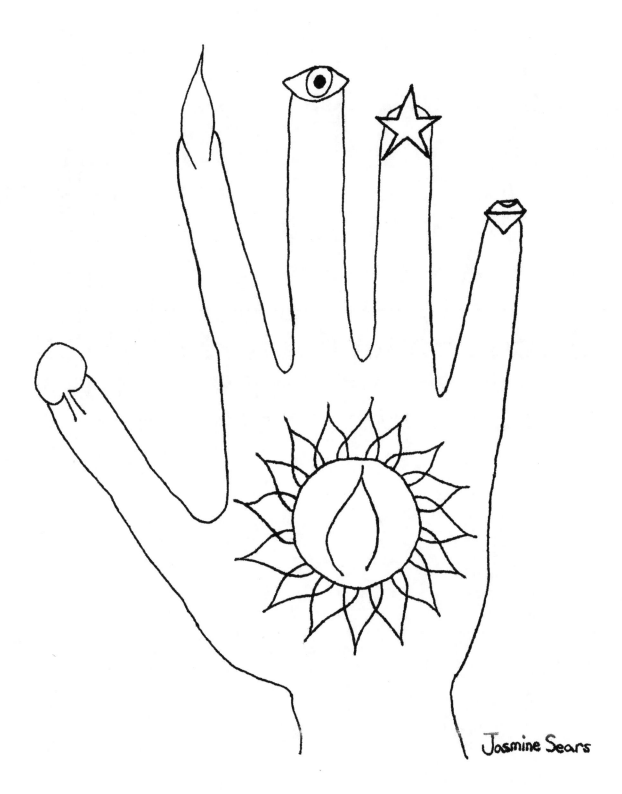

Jasmine Sears

Sledge Hammer and Brick Wall

REMOVING OBSTACLES / RESOLVING PROBLEMS

Life's Compass

DECISION MAKING / FINDING DIRECTION

N

W 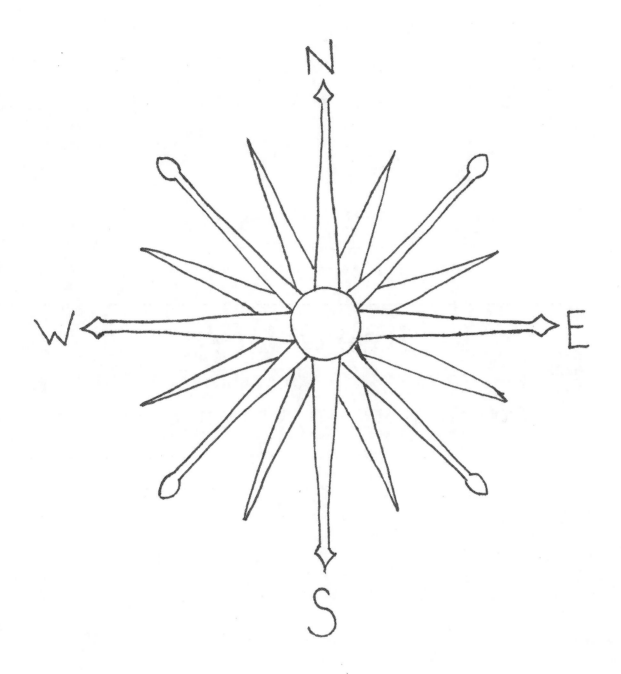 E

S

Chney Soria

Tree of Life

WORKING ON STRENGTH, GROWTH, COURAGE

Sunrise / Sunset

WORKING ON STABILITY, MATURITY, FAMILY

Candlelight

WORKING ON CLARITY, PURIFICATION, TRUTH

Jasmine Sears

Woman in Lotus Flower

BALANCING POWER, HEALTH, BEAUTY

Man with Chakras

Balancing Health, Strength, Power

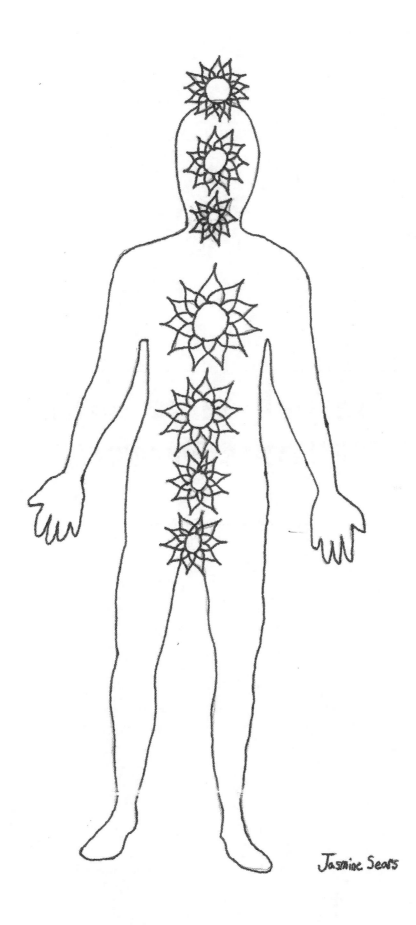

Jasmine Sears

Eternal Flame within Lotus Flower

Finding the Eternal Self

SECTION III

Translation Guides

Translation Guides

The first step in translating your coloring exercise is to look over your picture. There are clues in everything you did and even what you chose not to do. As you work through the translation, take time to think back on what was going through your mind when you were working on that particular spot on the page. The purpose of these exercises is to get as many data points from a work session as possible and then put them together into meaningful, actionable, messages.

Everything on the page is a clue to what your subconscious is trying to tell you. What you colored, and what you didn't color; the colors you used and where you used them; the type of stroke used, whether it was strong and bright or soft and light. Did the colors touch or overlap? Or were all the colors separated by some white space?

Each diagram has some specific symbolism. The main purpose is included in the title of each picture. In addition, each main purpose has subsets of inter-related areas of meaning. Your choice of which picture to color is your first clue as to what you want to work on. It can mean that you feel this is an area that is lacking and want to strengthen it. Or, it can mean that this is a problem area for you and you need resolution or clarity on how to correct it.

Each diagram has its own translation guidelines. The translation guidelines for shades and strokes are applicable for all of the diagrams; which is why they are discussed here.

SHADE AND STROKE OF COLOR

Pick a section of your picture that has color. Each color you placed on the picture has a personality. It has a specific stroke to it; harsh, soft, jagged, even, strong, or timid. Each type of stroke provides a specific clue to the state of mind and emotion surrounding the color and symbolism in this section of your picture. The same goes for the shade of color you chose. Is you color clear or muddy, bright or light? Let's talk about what these differences provide in the form of clues to understanding. A color can have multiple aspects, so in reading the below list select as many as apply. For example: a color can be clear and Loud, and strong, and have even strokes. And, each of these aspects will add to the specificity of the translation.

Clear shade   When a color is chosen to be portrayed as clear it means that you attempted to give it the purest form – unadulterated color. Now, your medium might not have let you succeed, but your intention is what counts. A clear color means that you yourself are clear on what your feelings are about this topic. You are being honest with yourself about your emotions on the subject.

Muddy Shade   A muddy color is when you have overlain a brown or black over the original color. So, if the base color is red then you would have put brown or black streaks, specs, or shadowing over it. When you give a color a muddy shade your inner-self is saying that there is lack of clarity around the topic. Either because you have too much baggage associated with the subject matter, or because you have mixed feeling or conflicting information. Either way, there needs to be further exploration on your emotions and stance on this subject because as it is now, you are not clear headed about it.

Loud/Bold   When a color is loud it has been drawn in such a way as to make a statement. Perhaps you went over the strokes multiple times to give it boldness. Just like the stroke, your emotions around this color and subject matter are very passionate; whether this is good or bad depends on the color itself. You want to shout out your opinion about this subject. You feel you are in the right and want to defend or evangelize your stance on the subject.

Pastel/Light   A pastel color is different from weak. The choice of a pastel or light color means that this is more a matter of fact feeling about the subject. There doesn't need to be a lot of discussion because you are sure about its correctness. You don't feel the need to "defend" or be "pushy" about your belief, it just is what it is and that is good enough for you.

Strong/Harsh   Strong is different from bold in that the pressure of the stroke on the page will have made a depression on the page. If you feel the backside of the paper you can trace your strokes by the bumpy terrain. This type of stroke indicates that you have pent up frustration or anger toward this subject. This is different from passion. With passion, the desire is to express the emotion not to oppress; this makes the stroke bold versus harsh. In a harsh stroke the desire is to force or pound the subject or emotion into submission. This comes across as vented emotion in the color. A suggested action is to re-color this area with pink or blue (love and tolerance) and purposely make the strokes softer, even, and gentle. This action sends the message back to your inner-self that you can deal with this emotion and subject in a more positive and benign manner.

Soft/Timid   These strokes are sometimes barely visible. The less visible they are the more

     MARTHA SORIA SEARS

afraid you are to express these emotions. You need to look at why you are feeling fearful in this area (see the symbol) or in expressing this emotion (see the color). Search your memory banks. Is there a history of events that have programmed this fear? Has your situation changed and now this fear is a habit? Brainstorm about how you can overcome the fear. The most extreme timid stroke I have seen was combined with trembling strokes. If this is a fear that is in response to a life situation, your picture is telling you that it is time to look for an organization or professional to help you through this.

Even strokes   An even stroke signifies that you are trying to be very level headed about this emotion or subject. Is this level headedness real or is it an attempt to hide your true feelings? Look deeper into the stroke. Is it a natural, smooth, even stroke? Or, is it a controlled stroke? If it is natural then this is an area that you have worked on already and you just need to acknowledge that you are at peace with it. If it is a controlled stroke, then this is an area where you are trying to tell yourself that you are at peace with it, but in reality you are denying your true feelings about it. Try again. Color it again and this time don't interfere with yourself. Let the true color be drawn and then translate it. A controlled stroke indicates that you are trying to bring about the translation that you want not the one that is true.

Jagged or   These strokes are similar to the harsh strokes, but the color actually looks
Sharp strokes   like arrows of color. Similar to the harsh strokes, your emotions about this subject are very strong and close to the surface. But, they are not necessarily negative emotions. What the stroke is saying is that you need action in this matter. You need to feel that you are doing something about this. You are ready to act. So, take a moment to discuss this with yourself. Are you already doing something about it but are not giving yourself credit for your efforts? Or, is the "doing something" out of your hands or realm of control? Is this something you need help with in order to put things into action? These strokes indicate that you want change and are ready to work for it but you feel like things aren't happening fast enough. You need a plan of action.

Each diagram's translation guide has suggestions throughout on how to diffuse specific areas being expressed in your picture. These are termed "Suggested Action". As the term states, these are suggestions on what to do to reverse, heal, or enhance a situation. There is a general type of exercise that can be applied to all diagrams. This exercise is described below.

OVERALL SUGGESTED ACTION

Now you have a better understanding of areas that you want to work on based on how your inner-self expressed the colors. You want to soothe or heal several areas, because by understanding you will be able to bring closure in your mind about them. In this case there is a soothing way to complete your session. First, follow whatever meditation was described in your diagram translation guide. Second, color the same diagram over but this time instead of letting your inner-self guide the session, have your conscious self lead. Make purposeful selections of colors, shades, and strokes based on what you want to heal, correct, or enhance. For example, if you had an area that you feel expressed weakness then use the color that describes what you want to feel and draw it in a clear, bold manner. And, so on, you develop the picture based on where you want to be in relation to the symbols. Again, the intention is not a pretty picture but rather a message back to your inner-self in the same language that it has communicated with you.

Mystic Hand

BALANCING LIFE'S ENERGIES

If you have chosen the Mystic Hand as your coloring exercise this in itself gives us a clue. The clue is that you have multiple areas of yourself that you want to address or enhance. You are ready to get to work and you are ready to multi-task. The Mystic Hand offers the opportunity for more dialogue than any other diagram in this book.

The symbolism of this diagram is that each of us is multi-faceted. Our lives are a continual balancing act of several aspects of our self. The topology of the hand can be used to identify areas in our life. Further meaning can also be derived from the symbols on each finger tip. Read through the below translation guide to understand what your drawing is expressing.

ONLY ONE COLOR ACROSS THE WHOLE PICTURE

This often indicates that there is one aspect of yourself dominating your whole outlook on life. You are having difficulty dealing with other things because this aspect has become so out of balance, maybe even out of control. Typically this happens with the colors described below. Your color is not described below? You can find where that color is talked about and apply that translation here using the same approach that is used below. If the color is not described any where else then think about what combination of colors it takes to get the color you have and use a combination of the translations of those colors. Remember to also work the shade and stroke into your translation.

The color that you chose tells you what aspect is out of balance:

Red   Your emotions are in control right now. You are having difficulty thinking straight because you are either feeling too much passion, fear, hurt, anger, or frustration. Your inner-self is venting this energy and needs to be acknowledged.

Suggested Action – give your body a way to express this pent up energy. Go for a walk, do some exercise, sing opera, or take a blank sheet of paper and fill it up with the strong bold strokes of red color. Now, that this energy has been vented, sit in a relaxed position and close your eyes. Take a slow deep breath and hold it for a few counts then slowly exhale. Repeat another two times, then breathing normally continue to sit in your relaxed position with your eyes closed. Now in your mind's eye see yourself sitting and surrounded by a soft white cool mist. Feel it refresh and calm you. Feel it heal your pain. With each inhale breathe in this refreshing, healing white mist. With each exhale breathe out the remaining red energy. After a few breaths you will notice that the red you are exhaling is softer and softer until it is more of a pink color. Thank your inner-self for communicating and working with you to bring back a balanced state. Count to three and open your eyes. Take a deep breath. You are done with the exercise.

Blue   You have concerns regarding your interpersonal self; this may be with family, friends, or people at work. You are feeling like one or more relationships are causing you stress, but because of who they are you feel you don't have much recourse for changing them or the situation.

Suggested Action – there are things that you need to say to this person or persons and for some reason you do not feel safe saying them. Take a sheet of paper and write them a letter saying everything you want to say to them. End the letter with what you would like this person to do or how you would like this relationship to change. Fold this letter and put it in an envelope and seal it. Label it with the person's name. Now take another piece of paper and write a letter to yourself about how you would like to resolve this relationship. If this was a perfect situation what would you do, what would you say? Write it all in this letter to yourself. Fold the paper and put it in an envelope, seal it and label it with your name. Now holding both letters in your hands, begin a meditation. Sit in a relaxed position and close your eyes. Take a slow deep breath and hold it for a few counts then slowly exhale. Repeat another two times. Now, breathing normally, continue to sit in your relaxed position with your eyes closed. In your mind's eye see yourself sitting in front of the person or persons to whom your letter is addressed. Tell them how you feel. Listen to what they have to say back to you. Continue the conversation with them. Be conscious to keep it on track. In other words, don't get bogged down in details or history or other topics that are not what you are here to resolve. Let the conversation take its course until it comes to a natural close. Now, tell them about what you want to fix in this relationship to the benefit of both of you. Say that you want it to be a healthy relationship. One that is enjoyable and mutually fulfilling. Thank them for working with you on reaching this goal. Thank your inner-self for communicating and working with you to bring back a balanced state. Count to three and open your eyes. Take a deep breath.

You are done with the exercise. Now destroy the two letters which ever way makes sense to you.

Special Note: sometimes the issue is that you need to end a relationship and you don't know how. In these situations the conversation should be focused around saying good bye. After the conversation, imagine that there is a string connecting both of you. Thank them for having been a part of your life and wish them peace and happiness. In your right hand see a pair of scissors. See yourself cutting the string that is connecting the two of you. Allow that image to transition into them leaving or disappearing. Thank your inner-self for communicating and working with you to bring back a balanced state. Count to three and open your eyes. Take a deep breath. You are done with the exercise. Now dispose of the two letters which ever way makes sense to you.

Green

You have concerns about your health or your physical being. If the shade of green is a yellowish green then you are concerned about illness or fearful that you will become ill. If the shade of green is a dark green, you are too focused on your physical self almost to the exclusion of other aspects of your life. Sometimes this happens when people become obsessed with their body and become addicted to exercise or diets. Essentially your source of stress is that your body is not what you want it to be and feel that you are failing in some way because of it.

Suggested Action – You need to think about your perceptions about yourself and give them a reality check. If you feel you are not healthy then go to the doctor. If you have been to the doctor and you checked out fine, but you can't let go of the feeling of being sick then you need to meditate on what is causing you to feel this way. If you are in good health but the stress is that your body does not look the way you think it should then your meditation should focus on where these expectations came from and why. In addition to the meditation you should also follow the below overall suggested action and go through that exercise every morning before starting your day until you feel your perceptions about your health and or body are back in balance with the rest of your life.

OVERALL SUGGESTED ACTION

You need to bring this aspect of yourself back in balance by taking the same picture and purposely coloring the hand an even color – using the same color that you have right now. But this time make your strokes soft and even, staying within the boundaries of the hand outline and respecting the outline of the symbols on the finger tips. Then using different colors begin to color the finger tip symbols. In this exercise you are looking to make this a very pretty picture. The pretty picture is your blueprint for the new way you want your life to be balanced, while still continuing to work on the area that is of concern.

COLOR OF FINGERS

If you colored all the fingers it means that you are being able to juggle all that life has presented you with. If the strokes of color are harsh, scratchy, and / or very loud and bright, you might have some concerns about keeping things going and in balance. Your stress stems from feeling that you can't let down your guard for a minute because without your constant attention things will become out of balance or fall to pieces. You need a rest.

If the strokes of color are soft and timid it means that your source of stress comes from feeling that you do not have enough meaning to all that you do. You may be very busy, but it is not an important type of busy. You are looking for more meaning to your life. Perhaps while you find this meaning to your life you could do some volunteer work, or take a class on something you've always wanted to learn.

If you only colored some fingers but not others then read on to see the meaning of each finger. The fingers you did not color simply mean that you are not as concerned about them right now, you have that area of life on "auto-pilot" for a while

You didn't color any of the fingers, but concentrated your color only on the symbols at the finger tips and palm. This means that you want to focus on "higher" things. Your stress comes from being bogged down with the day-to-day trivial busy tasks. You are stressed because you feel that you are not having the time you need to focus on more important things. You need to take a few days and focus on getting organized. Your lack of organization is putting you in a reactive mode to life which makes you feel that you are not in control.

THE MEANING OF THE FINGERS

The thumb symbolizes the practical side of life. This is the part of you that takes care of the survival level; such things as paying the bills, and keeping a stable job. When this finger has strong loud colors then there is stress in this area. You are meeting your responsibilities but are not happy in the process. Either you feel you work too hard at it or you are not enjoying the type of work you do. When this finger is soft and timid in color then you feel that this part of life is okay, not great, but this is not the time to change it.

The forefinger symbolizes your future. This is the part of you that is mapping the direction of your life. The tasks of this part of your life are planning, saving for the future, working toward a promotion at work, finding your spouse, planning a family. These are plans not dreams. When this finger has strong loud colors then you are stressed about not being able to meet these plans. For example, you are worried about not having enough money to send your children to school. When this finger has soft timid colors you feel that you will get by slowly but surely.

The middle finger symbolizes your aspirations and dreams. This is the part of you that extends beyond the life you have now to the life you wish you had. When this finger has strong loud colors it means that your stress comes from feeling that you will never reach your dreams. If this finger has soft timid colors you feel there is no point in dreaming because your chances of getting there are slim.

The ring finger symbolizes commitment. This commitment can mean marriage, school, career, or other important areas that you feel a sense of long term commitment to. If this finger has strokes of color that are not smooth and even, there is indication of stress due to turmoil in the areas of your commitment. If there are strong smooth strokes of color, you are very clear and strong in your commitment. If there are soft timid strokes, this is an area where you feel that though you are committed there might not be equal commitment from the other parties in the situation. If all you did was outline the finger with some color but left some blank areas in the center, you know you want this commitment but are not sure what it entails. Vise versa if your color does not touch the outline of the finger then you know what the commitment entails, and you want to be committed to it, but you are not ready to express it outwardly.

The pinky finger symbolizes the less visible but just as important aspects that make your life special. These might be the way you like to be acknowledged, or the way you like to express love, the way you organize yourself and others, in general this finger talks of the finishing touches you put on your life. Sometimes you see this finger colored very pretty even if the other fingers are not. This means that you are very proud of the special finishing touches you put on who you are. If the pinky is blank then it means you have not decided what you want your individuality expression to be. Another thing to note about the pinky is that it tends to speak more about outward expression of your taste and individuality rather than inward. So, fashion conscious people will have a very visible color on this finger. People who are more apt to be "nature" type of people have a more toned down color on their pinky.

THE COLORS USED ON THE FINGERS

Read the translation guide section for the specific finger then read the color below. By combining the guide for the specific finger, the shade and stroke, and the color you can get a more precise understanding of what your picture is expressing.

Red / Thumb   This signifies some frustration or anger toward the survival level. For example, concerns about paying the bills or anger at what you have to put up with in your work in order to make enough money to pay the bills. Read the significance of the thumb and see which area of the survival level is causing you this stress. **Suggested Action** – develop an action plan on how you can begin to improve your situation. If the anger is toward the type of work you are doing then your action plan should include something like training for the type of work you would like to do.

Red / Fore finger   This signifies that you are frustrated or angry at the direction of your life. The frustration might be not feeling you have control of where you are going, or not being able to decide on the direction of your life. Either way, your stress is in regards to feeling trapped or held back from your desired future. **Suggested Action** - assess where you are today and write down both the good things and the bad things about where you are today. This taking of inventory will help you see that not all is bad and some of the bad might be temporary. Once you have assessed where you are today, the next step is to identify where you want to be in five, ten, twenty years. What are your goals? Finally, what do you need to reach those goals? For example: more money, more education, a different set of relationships, etc. When you finish this map of where you are going you then need to reschedule or re-work your day-to-day life around it so that everyday you feel you are taking steps toward one of your goals. Manage your expectations to making baby steps weekly on one goal at a time. Once, you feel more confident that your plan is working you can adjust your expectations and your plan accordingly.

Red / Middle Finger   This finger also talks about the future, but unlike the forefinger, this finger talks more about your fantasies or dreams. Things you wish you could accomplish, but that are not real. If you have used red on this finger it means that your fantasy world is causing you stress. It means that what started out as a dream to temporarily escape your day-to-day life, has now turned into anger of "why can't I have that?" You need to do a reality check. If you really want that dream then establish goals toward it rather than just dreaming about it. What has happened is that you are confusing your dream with your direction in life and you need to re-assess which is which. Once you are clear on what a dream is and what an actual goal is, then you can adjust both appropriately.

Red / Ring Finger   This signifies stress over your commitments. Either you feel you are not being able to keep your commitments and are feeling angry or guilty about that. Or, you are feeling that something has changed in the situation and the commitment is not working out anymore. Red on this finger means that there needs to be dialogue with yourself and sometimes with those you have the commitment with, regarding the level of responsibility and reciprocation. Something needs to be adjusted, healed, and strengthened in this situation, either by you or the other party. Read the description of the ring finger to better understand what falls in the category of a commitment. Look to other fingers to get further clues as to what is causing this situation to no longer feel right. For example: if there is stress in the fore finger as well as in the ring finger, it might mean that you feel your current commitment is not in synch with your plans for the future. Before changing anything, ask yourself if the elements that are in conflict are mutually exclusive, or is it that you are assuming that the commitment is all inclusive when it might not be. An example of this can also be if the red extends beyond the boundary of the finger, this is a tell tale sign that your commitment has expanded its boundaries beyond what you had originally signed up for. Talk with the other party or parties to bring this situation back in balance.

Red / Pinky

This signifies that you are stressed out about your outward appearance. Something has made you feel that you do not come across in the way you want to be seen. This could be behavior, appearance, or social circle. This is also not necessarily that you feel you are not good looking enough or have rich enough friends. The dissatisfaction can go either way, in other words you might not be happy with the fact that people make assumption about you because you are too rich or too good looking and you want them to look beyond that but are not sure how to get them to do that. Think about stereotypes. Are you fighting a stereotype or are you trying to become one. You need clarity around who you are and who you want to portray because they are not in synch at this time.

Orange / Thumb

You are stressed over the amount of activity in your survival level – there is either too much going on or not enough. If the color is bright and bold then you are feeling that there is so much going on that you can't get your arms around it and are feeling frazzled by the whole thing. If the color is weak or does not fill up the whole thumb then you feel that your survival level has become dull and boring. You need to find something to bring fun back in your life. Orange is a physical color, so starting an exercise routine will help this area get back in balance quickly. Look to other fingers for further clues. For example: if your ring finger is showing some stress as well, then perhaps you feel that your survival level has taken the romance or passion out of your life.

Orange / Forefinger

This signifies that there is stress over the amount of action toward your future. Since Orange is a physical and survival level color it may mean that you are concerned that you are not being able to save enough money for your future plans. Or, you feel that your current job will not be able to provide enough money for you to meet your goals. From a physical aspect, it could speak to not taking enough action toward your future. In other words, you may feel like you have been lagging behind or that there are things getting in the way of progress toward your goals. Take inventory of where you are and re-assess your plans. It may be that your timelines for your goals are unrealistic and you need to make some adjustments to your plan.

Orange / Middle Finger This states that your creative aspect needs expression. You need to express your dreamy self. You feel that your creativity is stifled. **Suggested Action** - take a class in art, dance, drama, pottery, basket weaving, or any other expressive form to express your alter-ego, or your fantasy self.

Orange / Ring Finger This indicates that the level of activity in your commitments is a source of stress. For example, if you are planning a wedding or change of jobs, this finger would show up orange due to the stress of having so much to do in so little time. It is time to do a check-point and see if you are taking on too much yourself. Do you need to ask for help with the tasks at hand? If the color is muddy or very light and uneven, then the problem is more to do with feeling that there are too many obstacles to getting the job done. **Suggested Action** - get organized. By having a plan of action you can alleviate some of the stress. If this is an on-going area of stress, then perhaps taking a time management class will help.

Orange / Pinky Since orange is a survival level and physical color, orange on the pinky sometimes signifies that you are not getting enough physical activity and it is affecting your outward appearance or outlook. **Suggested Action** - do some stretching or take a walk to alleviate the immediate stress. Establish a regular exercise routine that preferably takes you outdoors; for example, walking, swimming, or jogging. The reason for the outdoors aspect is that the pinky is your outward finger so you are telling yourself that you need more activity and you need more outward expression.

Yellow / Thumb This signifies that you feel you need to exercise more intelligence when it comes to the survival level. For example, if you are an emotion shopper, this finger is saying that your stress comes from not spending your money more wisely.

Yellow / Forefinger Similar to the thumb, yellow on the forefinger talks about needing or wanting more wisdom when spending money. But the forefinger is talking about future, so the money we are talking about is in investments. It follows, that a light or muddy or uneven yellow on this finger speaks to being stressed over not having enough wisdom or knowledge to make sound investments. Bright or strong yellow means that you have been brainstorming around how to reach your future plans and formulating a plan of action. The stress felt in this situation has to do with feeling that you need to spend more time on applying this new knowledge and balancing this work for the future with your day-to-day survival. **Suggested Action** - develop your plan of action with a reality check approach. Then stick to the plan. When yellow in the forefinger gets strong it may be a challenge not to get carried away and want to pursue a get rich quick scheme.

Yellow / Middle Finger   Since the middle finger talks of your fantasy or dream self, it is not often that I see a yellow middle finger. The times that I have seen a yellow middle finger it stated that if you only knew more or had more education in a particular area you might be able to make this dream a reality. **Suggested Action** - do some research into this area. Maybe this dream is something you want to turn into a goal and actually work toward reaching it?

Yellow / Ring Finger   Since yellow is the color of intelligence or knowledge, a yellow ring finger is saying that your stress comes from either having too much knowledge about your area of commitment or not enough. For example, if you have just learned something about the party or parties in your committed area, the stress comes from feeling that now you need to react to this new information. If the yellow is a muddy color, you doubt the information and need to look further into it and either dismiss or verify it. If the yellow is weak, you feel you don't have enough information to make an intelligent decision about this commitment. **Suggested Action** - make a conscious effort to look at the information from all sides before reacting to the information.

Yellow / Pinky   This signifies that you feel you need to be more informed about how to present your outward appearance. For example, you feel frustration at not knowing enough about public speaking or enough about fashion to dress well, or you are stressed that you are going to a fancy dinner party and won't know how to behave. **Suggested Action** - identify the outward area that you feel lacking in and read up on it or take a class on it so that you feel more confident.

Green / Thumb   The shade of green on the thumb is very important because it talks about your health. If the green color is rich and dark then you feel that you are working on and taking care of your health; you have made health a strong focus in your life. If the shade is a yellowish or brownish green then your stress comes from being concerned about your health or the health of someone in your family.

Green / Forefinger

This signifies that there is concern over your future health. The shade mainly talks more specifically about what type of concern. For example, if the shade is yellowish or muddy, you are concerned about a health situation that you feel may take a turn for the worse in the near future. If the color is a dark rich green, you are concerned over heading off some type of illness in the future. You are concerned that you are at risk for some type of illness and are working on prevention. **Suggested Action** - do some research about your health so that you are not so stressed about it. Once you understand what your real risks are, you can develop a more structured approach to prevention or healing and in this way alleviate some of the stress in this area.

Green / Middle Finger

This signifies stress over health and how health is what is making your dreams unreachable. You are feeling frustrated that your health is an obstacle to achieving more in your life and therefore feel you have had to lower your goals and make compromises. **Suggested Action** - do some research and see if you are making assumptions about your health that are incorrect. Look for ways to be more in control of your health so that you feel you can work toward a better health and possibly re-establish some of your bigger goals.

Green / Ring Finger

This is a very important clue as to how you are reacting to your commitments. Your inner-self is telling you that your health, whether good or bad, is dependent on your commitment. Too often this means that your stress level over work or family have reached a point that is having an adverse effect on your health. **Suggested Action** - work on releasing and venting. Read the suggested action described under All One Color / Red. In addition, look to other fingers of the hand. Where is there red? This is a clue as to the specifics of what about this commitment is frustrating you.

Green / Pinky

This signifies that you feel your health condition to be affecting your outward appearance. If the color is muddy or yellowish, you feel that whatever ailment you have is affecting your looks and it is very visible to people around you. This may be true or this may be only your perception. Either way, you should do some research into what options are available to you for correcting the situation. If the color is a dark rich green, the stress comes from knowing what you need to do for a healthier outward appearance but are not acting on it or feeling frustrated at not making enough progress with it. Bottom line, you are self-conscious about your appearance and it is causing you stress. **Suggested Action** - perform a reality check to see whether your assumptions are true or just your own perception. Develop an action plan on how to get to the state of health that you want.

Blue / Thumb	This signifies that you are not happy with the level of social activity in your day-to-day life. Perhaps you feel that your focus on the survival level means not having enough time for friends or family. You are feeling alone and don't like it.
Blue / Forefinger	This signifies that you have stress over the type of people you are surrounded by. Either you feel they are holding you back or they are not the type of people that will help you get to where you want to be. If the color is dark and bold, it means that you feel that people will be an important element to your success and the stress comes from realizing how much work it means to keep relationships strong. If the color is light or muddy, you are concerned that the people aspect of your life is not healthy and will interfere with your future. You may be feeling that you have relationships that you have outgrown and don't know how to end them without a negative repercussion.
Blue / Middle Finger	The stress here comes from realizing that you use your social circle to live out your fantasy. Your concern is that your relationships are not real – they are too superficial.
Blue / Ring Finger	The stress expressed here is due to commitments. You are balancing relationships that you feel need a lot of work. For example, if you may be a newly married and feel that building healthy relationships with in-laws is turning out to be more work than you anticipated. Or you may be in a work situation where you have realized that in order to solidify your position you need to participate in relationships that you normally would not have.
Blue / Pinky	This signifies that you have some stress over how your relationships view you. If this color is muddy, the stress comes from feeling judged by either your family or friends. If the color is strong and bold, much of your self-confidence comes from your family and friends and this in itself is putting pressure on you.
Purple / Thumb	This signifies the spiritual aspect of your family or day-to-day life is of concern to you. Either you feel there is not enough spiritual focus or there is too much for your comfort. Other times that purple comes up on the thumb is when there is spiritual conflict within the day-to-day life; for example, when one person in the family has a different belief system than the rest.
Purple / Forefinger	This says that you are concerned about keeping a spiritual focus in your future plans. For example, if you are starting to see your big goals getting closer and you are feeling temptation to compromise your spiritual beliefs, this will cause some spiritual stress. If the color

is a deep, clear, and strong purple, then this speaks to a calling for spiritual work and the stress comes from having to make a decision about this calling.

Purple / Middle Finger   This speaks of your visionary self. Having purple show up in the middle finger says that stress comes from your intellect and intuition not been in balance. Either you have been experiencing some intuitive impressions and aren't sure what they mean, or are having difficulty accepting that you have intuitive abilities.

Purple / Ring Finger   This speaks of conflicts between your spiritual beliefs and what you are being asked to do by your commitment situation. This may happen when you have an inter-faith marriage and the differences are causing some stress. Or, this may happen when you are finding that you are being asked to do something at work or school that is contrary to your spiritual beliefs. In general, you are feeling that an important situation is putting you at odds with your spiritual beliefs.

Purple / Pinky   This signifies that you feel your spiritual beliefs are either too visible to others or you are trying to make your beliefs more outwardly visible. Sometimes, this happens when you have found a new faith and are so excited about it that you want to evangelize others. Or the reverse, someone in your social circle is trying to impose their spiritual beliefs on you and you are feeling stressed about it.

Pink / Thumb   The stress being expressed here is in the romantic part of your life. Either you are stressed over a romantic interest or you are feeling the lack of romance in your life. A muddy pink indicates problem with a romantic relationship.

Pink / Forefinger   This indicates that your future plans are in some way at odds with your romantic life. You may feel that your romance is not part of what you see for your future. Or, you may be feeling that in order to reach your future goals you are being asked to sacrifice a romance. **Suggested Action** - assess your future plans and set priorities on what is more important to you – your romance or your goals? Do they have to be in conflict? Or, are you making assumptions without letting the other party or parties have input into these decisions?

Pink / Middle Finger   There is some fantasizing going on about a romance. This romantic dream is causing stress in other areas of your life because you may be having difficulty separating the dream from reality. Sometimes, this shows up when a relationship is over but you are having difficulty moving on because you are still thinking that the person will return.

Pink / Ring Finger	This signifies that commitment and romance are in conflict. If the pink is clear and bold, the conflict is that the romance is so strong that it is not allowing enough focus on other areas of the relationship. If the commitment is a career, you are so in love with what you are doing that you may be overlooking other areas of the career that will cause problems later on. If the color is muddy or the strokes are jagged, this speaks of conflict between a situation you have committed to and a separate situation that you are in love with.
Pink / Pinky	The stress you feel is due to falling in love with superficial aspects of situations or people. Your inner-self is telling you that you need to look deeper before falling in love.
Brown / Thumb	This signifies that your stress is coming from discipline; either too much or not enough in your day-to-day life. If the color is uneven or turbulent, it speaks to your own discipline not being what it needs to be and this is causing you stress. If the color is strong and dark, you feel that you may be too disciplined and this causes stress on yourself and others.
Brown / Forefinger	The stress expressed here is that you may not have the discipline you feel you need in order to reach your goals. So you are expressing frustration with yourself about this lack of discipline. Take a check-point to see if you are pushing yourself too hard. Are your goals or timelines realistic? This expression of stress is saying that you may feel out of synch with yourself when it comes to your future plans.
Brown / Middle Finger	This signifies that you are concerned over your own fantasies or dreams. You may be feeling that you are spending too much time dreaming and not enough time doing. Or, you may be feeling a lack of dreaming and need to find a way to escape every now and then.
Brown / Ring Finger	The discipline required by your commitment is starting to weigh you down. You may also be feeling that the discipline that is being required of you is not fair or reciprocated by the other party or parties. Your stress may be telling you that it is time to re-negotiate the rules of this commitment.

THE FINGER TIP COLORS AND SYMBOLS

Sometimes the symbols get colored the same as the finger they are on which means that the important message has to do with the meaning of the finger and not so much with the symbol. But where the symbol is colored differently from the finger it is on, then your inner-self is making a statement that you may want to look into. The color translation of these symbols is somewhat more basic than for the fingers. It is suggested that you look for the combination of color(s) and symbol to get a more complete translation.

Red When red appears on one of the symbols, you are experiencing frustration in regards to the aspect represented by the symbol. For example, a red tree speaks to frustration with the level of stability in your life. Another interpretation of red would be that you are so passionate about this area that you are frustrated that you can't do more with it. For example, a red flame may mean that you are very passionate about what you want to dedicate your life to but are feeling that you are unable to act on it. This can be seen when someone has a cause they want to fully support but feel that taking care of the survival level is not allowing them to have enough money or time to dedicate to their cause.

Orange This color speaks to the level of activity in the area represented by the symbol is not to your liking and thus is causing some stress. For example, an orange flame says you feel you are not doing enough for your cause. Sometimes this happens when your expectations of yourself are unrealistic so no matter how much you do you always feel you need to do more and this generates stress for you. The difference between red and orange is that red speaks to your dedication and orange speaks to the level of action.

Yellow This color is telling you that you want and need more information in order to feel at peace with this aspect of yourself. You are trying to understand yourself. You have acknowledged that there is an item to work on and now you need more information for the next step. You are in search of something to do with the area represented by the symbol.

Green This signifies that the health aspect of the area represented by the symbol is out of synch. For example, a green tree means you are healing the family unit or working on enhancing stability in your life. If your gem is green, it means you are a natural healer. If the green is mixed with yellow, you need or want information or training on how to heal.

Blue This signifies that the people aspect is what is in conflict or what you need to work on when it comes to the area represented by the symbol. For example, a blue gem is telling you that your natural ability to work with people is an area that is causing you some stress. This may be because people keep coming to you for help and you are having difficulty saying "no" or are feeling frustrated that you can't help them.

Purple This speaks of a spiritual nature. For example, people who have a calling for being spiritual leaders tend to have a purple gem. If you have a purple tree, you are working on the spiritual aspect of your family or are trying to establish stability in your life by way of religion.

Silver	This color often speaks to money being the area of concern. For example, if your eye is silver, you may be at odds with either paying for intuitive help or you yourself are intuitive and are at odds with charging for your services. Another example is a silver star which speaks to aspirations of being wealthy.
Black	This color is often placed on a symbol when the area represented by the symbol is something you don't want to deal with right now. Other times, it is an area in which you are in denial about and this denial is causing you stress. For example, a black eye would say that you are in denial about your intuitive abilities. Another example is a black tree would mean that there is something that is out of balance in your family or level of stability but you do not want to face it just yet.
Brown	This color speaks to the level of discipline in the area represented by the symbol. Your inner-self is saying that your level of discipline is causing you stress.
Tree	We look for a sense of belonging, stability, and family as portrayed by the tree.
Flame	We all need something to feel passionate about, something that makes our life worth living, something that we can dedicate ourselves to simply because we believe in it; this is symbolized by the flame.
Eye	The eye is an important symbol in many cultures, although it does not mean the same across those same cultures. In this picture, the eye symbolizes your intuition and connection to other realms.
Star	The star is also an important symbol in many cultures. For this picture, the star symbolizes your aspirations, dreams, and who you would be if you could.
Gem	The gem symbolizes those aspects of yourself that are pure and idealistic. No matter how much of ourselves we compromise in today's negotiated life, each of us has a line that we will not cross because it is our connection to our pure and untarnished self; this is symbolized by the Gem.
Lotus Flower	The Lotus flower at the center of the palm symbolizes the center of your existence. This speaks of areas you are working on that extend beyond this current life. This also speaks to aspects of other lives that may be acting on this one, in a sense it speaks of what karma you are working on.
Flame	The flame within the lotus flower tells you what your specific connection to your higher self is. What aspect of yourself is the doorway to your higher consciousness? This may be a personality trait that you have kept throughout all of your lifetimes.

Background   If you chose to fill in the background of the picture, your inner-self is speaking about external factors. This is the part of life that is acting on you, but is out of your realm of control. This can be politics, world events, the socio-economic arena, and other areas of life that you are concerned with. If you left the background blank, then your focus right now is on you and what you can do about yourself.

Sledge Hammer and Brick Wall

REMOVING OBSTACLES / RESOLVING PROBLEMS

If you have chosen the sledge hammer and brick wall your internal dialogue is focused around removing obstacles to a situation, or resolving a problem. This exercise is designed to identify the source of the obstacles. In addition, it speaks to what aspect of your self has the ability to remove or resolve the situation.

The first area to analyze is where you started to color. Did you first color the sledge hammer? Or, did you first color the wall? This is a very important thing to understand about your situation because it speaks to you approach toward your situation. It gives clues as to where you are focusing. It may even give you clues on how you approach your life in general. So, be honest with yourself. Where did you start your picture?

SLEDGE HAMMER AS THE STARTING POINT

If you started your picture with the sledge hammer, it signifies that you are focused on finding a way to break through the obstacles and problems. You want to find the answer and get to work.

Did you start with the head of the hammer? If so, you are more focused on swift action rather than a controlled process. It is understandable that some situations get to such an overwhelming point that we begin to look for the "Off Switch". Generally though, there is no switch or instant fix. Typically, it is a consistent solid approach that gets the job done. The action you need to take to resolve the situation is very important. By making sure that you are also focusing on the approach and using it in a controlled manner you are mitigating the risk of starting an action / reaction cycle. Focusing more on the process also gives you a tool that can be used over and over again to solve other situations. In summary, focusing on the action gives you a one-time solution, focusing on the process increases your ability to solve problems across the board.

Did you start with the handle of the hammer? If so, you are more focused on the process rather than the action. People who start with the handle tend to have a "Big Picture" approach to the situation. You want to fix the current situation but you also want to learn how to solve problems in general and learn how to prevent this situation from happening again. There is not as much sense of "do it now" but rather a sense of "do it right".

BRICK WALL AS THE STARTING POINT

Did you start with the brick wall? If so, you are so focused on the problem that you might not be seeing the answer. You need to take a step back and look at the whole situation. This will give you the opportunity to see what tools you have at your disposal.

Did you draw a crack in the wall? If so, you already see areas in the situation that can be resolved with little effort. You see the weakness in the problem and are looking for validation that it is the correct place to strike. If you colored up and down the whole crack first, you are being cautious and trying to investigate to see what type of repercussions or fallout would result from removing the obstacle or resolving the situation. You feel there is an inter-dependency that may not be obvious to others. But, you feel it is a risk that needs to be explored deeper prior to any action.

BACKGROUND AS THE STARTING POINT

Did you start by coloring the background? If so, you feel that the obstacle or problem is only a symptom of a much larger issue. You feel this is an issue that may be out of the realm of your control. Ask yourself whether you are being honest about this. Sometimes blaming the obstacle or problem on external factors is a way to justify not dealing with the problem at hand. You need to ask yourself, is this really out of my control or do I just not want to deal with it?

OVERALL SUGGESTED ACTION

After you have translated the rest of your picture, do the exercise again. This time purposefully start your coloring with the handle of the sledge hammer, then the head of the hammer, then draw the cracks in the wall, and finally the bricks starting from the cracks outward. This exercise is outlining the process of attacking the situation from a position of strength and control – the handle. When you get to the wall, you are focusing on the cracks which are a symbolism for the parts in the situation which are ready to be resolved. By starting at the situation's weakest point, you further strengthen your position and allow the situation to start to resolve itself from within.

Make a conscious effort to select the colors based on what you want to enhance and correct in your situation using the color translation guide.

ONLY ONE COLOR ACROSS THE WHOLE PICTURE

This often indicates that the obstacle or problem is actually one aspect that is so out of balance that it is having a negative impact on everything else. Keep in mind that very few things in life are so simple that they only have one aspect to them. It may be that what you are seeing is the main area being affected by the problem. Then once you work through the emotions around that affected area you will be able to get more information about what the situation entails. For an understanding of what this affected area is, read the color translations below.

Your color is not described below? You can find where that color is discussed and apply that translation here using the same approach that is used below. If the color is not described any where else, then think about what combination of colors it takes to get the color you have and use a combination of the translations of those colors. Remember to also work the shade and stroke into your translation.

The color that you chose tells you what aspect is out of balance:

Red

There is so much anger, frustration, and emotion around this obstacle / situation that you are not being able to see straight. This emotion is blocking you from finding resolution. **Suggested Action** – give your body a way to express this pent up energy. Go for a walk, do some exercise, sing opera, or take a blank sheet of paper and fill it up with the strong bold strokes of red color. Now that this energy has been vented, sit in a relaxed position and close your eyes. Take a slow deep breath and hold it for a few counts, then slowly exhale. Repeat another two times, then breathing normally continue to sit in your relaxed position with your eyes closed. In your mind's eye see yourself sitting and surrounded by a soft white cool mist. Feel it refresh and calm you. Feel it heal your pain. With each inhale breathe in this refreshing, healing white mist. With each exhale breathe out the remaining red energy. After a few breaths, you will notice that the red you are exhaling is softer and softer until it is more of a pink color. Thank your inner-self for communicating and working with you to bring back a balanced state. Count to three and open your eyes. Take a deep breath. You are done with the exercise. Now, go back and repeat the coloring exercise. If you find yourself using more colors then you know that you have overcome the emotional hurdle and are ready to get more information about your situation. If you are still using one color, work through that color again and keep repeating the exercise until you start to see more colors. Since most problems / obstacles / situations have many facets, you should eventually see several colors on the wall.

Orange

This is saying that the situation is threatening the survival level – job, finances, food and shelter. The fact that the whole picture is orange says that your fear of this threat is not allowing you to see beyond the problem itself. The suggested action is similar to the one for red. Follow the meditation and then work the exercise again. **Suggested Action** – give your body a way to express this pent up fear and anxiety. Go for a walk, do some exercise, sing opera, or take a blank sheet of paper and fill it up with the strong bold strokes of color, any color you want. Now, that this energy has been vented, sit in a relaxed position and close your eyes. Take a slow deep breath and hold it for a few counts, and slowly exhale. Repeat another two times, then breathing normally continue to sit in your relaxed position with your eyes closed. In your mind's eye see yourself sitting and surrounded by a soft white cool mist. Feel it refresh and calm you. Feel it heal your fear. With each inhale, breathe in this refreshing, healing white mist. With each exhale, breathe out the orange energy. After a few breaths you will notice that the orange you are exhaling is softer and softer until it is more of a yellow color. Thank your inner-self for communicating and working with you to bring back a balanced state. Count to three and open your eyes. Take a deep breath. You are done with the exercise. Now, go back and repeat the coloring exercise. If you find yourself using more colors, you know that you have overcome the emotional hurdle and are ready to get more information about your situation. If you are still using one color, then work through that color again and keep repeating the exercise until you start to see more colors. Since most problems / obstacles / situations have many facets, you should eventually see several colors on the wall.

Yellow   This is saying that you are caught up in analysis paralysis. You have too much information you are trying to use to resolve the issue. You need to simplify your variables. Look at the key items and put the minor details to the side for a moment. **Suggested Action** - group your information in different categories to help make sense of the whole thing. Prioritize both the information and your expectations of how the situation will be resolved. Get organized and put some structure to your information. Next, repeat the exercise but this time purposefully color the hammer handle yellow and the hammer head orange. This is a statement that you need to act, and act intelligently.

Green   Often when green covers the whole page, the person is dealing with a health issue. **Suggested Action** – focus your translation on the colors of the hammer. If the hammer is also green, see if it is a different green. If there is a difference in shades of green, then go to the translation of shades and strokes to get more information on what your inner-self is saying about this health condition. You may be telling yourself that a different approach to your health is necessary. Maybe it is time for a second opinion on the situation. If the hammer is blank, or the same green as the wall, then repeat the exercise focusing only on the hammer.

Blue   The people aspect of the situation is complicating the issue. The people you are dealing with are the real situation that needs attention, and what you thought was the problem is only an extension or result of it. By dealing with the people involved you will be able to make progress on resolving this situation.

Suggested Action – analyze the situation. Ask yourself "How do these people benefit from this situation?" This will help you understand where they are coming from. Then ask yourself "How can I show them the benefit of resolving this situation?" The proverbial "Win / Win" approach is what is needed here.

Brown   You are so disciplined that you are not allowing yourself to "think out of the box." This situation is unlike others you have dealt with. Yet, you want to resolve it in the same old way. You need to activate your creative side in order to brainstorm a solution. **Suggested Action** – repeat the exercise. This time, purposefully color the hammer purple – any shades of purple you like. Purple symbolizes your creative and spiritual self. You are opening up your intuition. You are opening yourself up to other options. Now as you color the rest of the picture you should start getting other clues that will help you brainstorm a solution.

OVERALL SUGGESTED ACTION

You need to allow yourself to look at the situation from other and all angles. Repeat the exercise. This time make an effort to use more colors. At first you might feel like you are only attracted to the same color you used before. Honor this feeling by still using the color in a small area of the picture, then put it to the side so that it is no longer an option to select it. Continue with the exercise using other colors. Start with the hammer handle, followed by the hammer head, followed by the crack on the wall, followed by the bricks starting from the crack and working outward.

SECTIONS AND COLORS

If your picture has each brick a different color then you recognize that this situation you are working to resolve has many facets. Each color you used is a clue to one of these facets. Following is a translation guide for each color by section of the picture. If the specific color you used is not mentioned in a section, you can apply the same type logic and use the translation of the color where it is mentioned elsewhere. If the color is not mentioned any place, then use the combination of colors that would make up the color that you used.

Hammer Handle The handle has stripes leading up to the neck and head of the hammer. If you colored all the stripes the same, then focus on the translation of that color as the approach or aspect to work on for the process to resolution. If you colored each stripe a different color, then start at the bottom and work up. What you are saying to yourself is that there is a series of steps in the process to resolution and they need to be taken in a specific chronological sequence.

Red	A red handle says that your process needs to keep emotions in check. The process will bring out emotions but you need to be in control of them.
Orange	An orange handle says that the process needs to include a plan of action that protects or covers your survival level. In other words you need to have contingency plans.
Yellow	The yellow in the handle is saying that you need to think through the process carefully because this is your strongest tool. Using your intelligence, using knowledge, and having information will be what gets you to a successful conclusion.
Green	The green handle is saying that you need to make sure you are in good health as you proceed with this battle. This may speak to a long hard battle and you will need your strength and stamina.
Blue	This color in the handle means that your plan of action needs to include other people. This might be allies or people you work with, or hired professionals. These are not necessarily people you love – those will show up under pink.
Purple	This means that your process for resolving the situation needs to include a spiritual element. You need to make sure that you are adhering to your ethics and belief system. In order to resolve the situation, you will need to stay firm to your beliefs.
Pink	This color speaks of using love as part of the process to resolution. In other words, the situation should not be allowed to turn ugly. Make sure that you act with love and find a solution that does not harm the other party.
Silver	When this color shows up in the handle it means that the process to resolution may involve money. This sometimes is in the form of hiring a professional.
Brown	This color in the handle says that you will need to be very structured and disciplines in your approach of this situation. If you approach it without a well structured plan you will fail. So, spend time planning and stick to the plan.
Black	This is a very important color to heed when it shows up on the handle. It means that you need to be discreet with your plans. Don't go bragging or even talk about your plans on how to resolve this situation. Letting your plan be known to early in the game will work against you.

Hammer Head The hammer head has three sections, the neck, and two sides. The neck symbolizes the element that needs to be present to make sure that what actions you take are positioned properly for success. Each of the sides of the hammer head can be separate actions. If you colored both sides the same then there is one main action to take.

MARTHA SORIA SEARS

Red	There must be passion in the action you take. If you don't feel strongly about what you are to do, then you will not succeed. Your strength comes from your emotions about resolving this situation.
Orange	Your action will be in the area of the survival level. Sometimes this means that in order to resolve the problem, you may need to move, find a new job, or transfer from your department to another. The action you are contemplating may affect your survival level.
Yellow	Your action will need to be well thought out. Your strength is your intelligence and the information you have. This is a situation where "knowledge is power."
Green	The action you take will require achieving good health or helping someone achieve good health.
Blue	The action you are contemplating involves leveraging relationships. These are most likely work relationships, since people you love would show up under pink. If you have both blue and pink together, it speaks to using family or romantic relationships to solve the problem.
Purple	Your action will be a spiritual one. Your strength comes from knowing that what you are doing will be a "good" action. You are doing it for the greater good not just for yourself.
Pink	Your source of strength in action is love. You will be acting out of love or will be taking action with someone you love as a partner in the process.
Silver	The action you are looking at will be one with money. Your action may be to pay for the situation to be resolved; for example, as in paying for a settlement.
Brown	Your action is one that stems from tradition or discipline. It is a calculated action not an emotional one.
Black	Your action will need to be in secret. You will be the one acting to resolve the situation, but others can not know that it is you.

Crack in the Wall If you chose to draw a crack in the wall, this speaks to the weaknesses you have already spotted in the obstacle / problem / situation. This is where you should strike first. This will be the most effective point and may even start a chain reaction to dissolving the whole situation. If the crack has several colors, you are in luck because there are multiple weak areas which may mean the whole obstacle is ready to fall of its own or with very little effort on your part.

Red	Fear can make this situation crumble. Red speaks to strong emotions like fear, anxiety, frustration, or anger. Sometimes it also speaks to passion. If the color is clear and bold, you are dealing with a situation where the other party is very passionate about their position or stance. By being aware of this, you can diffuse the situation by presenting an option that respects their beliefs. If the color is muddy, it is warning you that the other party's own anger will be their undoing. Your reaction to the other party needs to be a calm one so that you don't get sucked into the negative emotion and aftermath.
Orange	This color speaks to the survival level. The situation you are facing involves your job, finance, or home. Look to the hammer colors to see how to best address the situation and mitigate the risk to these areas. When there is an orange crack, solving the situation may mean a change in the survival level – such as a new job or a change of residence. Further more, since the color is already in the crack, it may mean that this change is already in the works.
Yellow	When this color shows up in the crack, the undoing of the situation will come by way of knowledge. This may mean that educating someone to the facts is what is needed to resolve the situation. Conduct a review of what data points you have. Understanding what information to use and how to use it needs some analysis. Look to the hammer colors for additional clues.
Green	When the crack is green, the situation will be resolved as a result of correcting a health issue. This may be your health or the health of the other party. For example, if the other party has an illness that is causing a problem at work or with your relationship, then by helping them find help for their problem will help resolve the situation that is affecting you. I remember seeing this in a person's picture that had a very difficult situation at work. After further investigation, it turned out that the co-worker had a problem with a disorder that was causing them to behave erratically and was alienating several key people. This alienation was affecting a key project. By working with the person to go to the doctor and get checked, their behavior changed, the relationships were mended, and the project was able to get back on track.
Blue	A blue crack means that the way to start to resolve this situation relies on people. You may not be aware that you have allies that can help you with this situation. Work on your relationships.
Purple	When this color shows up in the crack, your own belief system and ethics will get you through this situation. This picture is telling you to have faith.
Pink	This color is saying that love will conquer all. By acting from a position of love and acting with love you will be able to resolve this situation.
Silver	This color is saying that the situation is ready to be resolved and you might even come out of it with some money. I often see this when the situation is

a lawsuit and the person is about to be awarded a settlement. Now, if both the crack and the hammer head are silver then you will need to spend some money to get money.

Brown	This color speaks to using tradition and discipline to resolve the situation.
Black	This is making the statement that the situation will be resolved, but you may not be aware of the things that are going on behind the scenes to resolve it.

Bricks As stated earlier in this chapter, each brick signifies a specific aspect of the situation and should be treated as a clue to the overall resolution. Some people feel that there is a correlation between the number of bricks in each color. I have not found this to be consistently true. So you will need to use your own judgment. If you have more bricks of the same color than another, ask yourself whether that means that that aspect is bigger or stronger than the other.

Red	In general, red speaks of emotions. If the red is clear, the emotion is more of a passion like a belief in a cause. If the red is darker with brown in it, more like a brick color, then the emotion is that of anger, frustration, fear, or anxiety. Be aware that part of the situation you are facing has a lot of emotion around it and it will be difficult to get around that. You might consider reading or taking a class on negotiations and or conflict resolution as part of your plan of action.
Orange	This color speaks of the survival level; such as job, finances, and home. Be aware that part of the situation you are facing may be threatening the survival level. This would mean that you need to proceed carefully and quickly so that you are the one that calls the shots as this situation unfolds. If the bricks that are orange are close to the cracks, then you might want to include some alternate plans for job and home as part of a plan "B".
Yellow	This color speaks of knowledge and information. Take the time to do your due diligence. There is something you don't know and it could trip you up. This is definitely a sign to plan each step toward resolution carefully so that you don't get caught in cross-fire or don't end up causing problems in other areas. If the color is a muddy yellow, then be aware that someone might be putting out misinformation. Sometimes, this is seen in situations where someone is planting information to deflect blame or responsibility. Muddy yellow means that you need to verify every piece of information, and you may need to do some damage control to clear your name.
Green	This color does not show up very often in bricks, but when it does it speaks to health. I remember one time that I worked on a picture where there were green bricks scattered over a blue and orange wall. The blue and orange meant that the person's job was suffering due to the relationship with their boss. The

solution to the problem ended up being transferring departments. It turned out that the new department was in a separate building and as soon as they started working in this other building their allergies cleared up. So, the green bricks on the wall meant that there was more to the situation than just a bad boss but also an environment that was bad for their health.

Blue   This color speaks to the situation having a people aspect to it. Part of the problem or obstacle is the people involved. So by learning how to deal with those people you will be able to start to resolve the situation. Look to the hammer for clues on how to deal with these people.

Purple   This situation includes an ethics aspect. The situation might be around a conflict of ethics or beliefs and how you will resolve them. Look to other colors to get a more specific read. If the purple is next to blue then the clue is that by understanding the belief system and ethics of the people involved you will be able to see a way to resolving the situation.

Pink   This color appears when the situation involves a romantic aspect. This means that the obstacle or problem has to do with someone you are romantically involved with or deals with your romantic life in general. It can also mean that you are making decisions about other aspects of your life based on your romantic feelings for someone.

Silver   This color speaks to the financial aspect of the situation. If there is silver both on the wall and in the background then your situation is linked in some way to the economy or financial markets. If there is orange or red in the wall as well, be cautious because your inner-self is concerned that you are placing yourself at financial risk. If the crack is red and the bricks are silver, it means that fear in the marketplace is going to have an impact on the financial situation.

Brown   Brown bricks say that the situation has an aspect of tradition and discipline. In other words, the situation is based on or concerned about the status-quo. Look to the color of the crack to see what this status-quo is afraid of and you might be able to diffuse their fear and help them get through this situation.

Black   This color comes up when there are unknowns in the situations that may impact the outcome. There is something that is being kept a secret that may be coming down the pike and you need to be ready for it. I see this mostly in situations where there is a merger or acquisition being planned but not announced, the situation needs to wait for that information to become public before being able to act or else the action may be overturned by the upcoming events. If there is black, you might want to see if your timing is off, you may want to wait a bit while you gather more intelligence and then re-assess the situation.

Background if you have colors in the background, either surrounding the wall or the hammer, you feel that there are external factors acting on this situation (wall) or on your ability to resolve the situation (hammer). If the colors go right up to the boundary of the wall or hammer, you feel there is a real connection and any action needs to take this into consideration. If the color stops short of the diagram's boundaries, it is only an aspect of influence and should be treated as something to keep in the back of your mind. As in other diagrams, the background talks of external factors which are outside the realm of your control. In this particular diagram these external factors may be present to remind you to manage your expectations of how much of this situation you can resolve yourself and how much of it you may need to learn to work around.

Red	The external factor you sense is the emotions of others when it comes to this situation. They may not necessarily have a direct impact on the situation, but you do need to be aware that there will be an emotional response from others as you resolve this situation.
Orange	The external factor here is that of the survival level. This means you believe that if you resolve this situation there will be an impact to your survival level. The survival level deals with your job, finances, and home. An example of when I have seen this is where the obstacle being resolved was an obstacle to a promotion. When the obstacle was removed and the promotion was achieved, it came with a requirement for re-location. This was a factor that would have caught the person by surprise had they not already been given a heads up that there would be some impact to that aspect of their life.
Yellow	This color speaks to the external factor being additional knowledge. I'd like to share two examples of when I have seen this in pictures. In one example, the yellow external color was directly touching the green wall. The translation was that when dealing with their illness they would come into additional information that they did not expect to have. The result was that in working through the illness they had to do some family research and found that the illness was hereditary. This person had never known that anyone else in the family had suffered from the same illness. In the second example, the yellow external color was around the silver wall and orange hammer. The translation was that the way to resolve the obstacle to a financial situation was through changes in the survival level – new job or a move of residence. There was a new job with much better pay but it required some additional training.
Green	The external factor here has to do with health. Depending on the shade of green, you may be sensing that by resolving the situation your health will improve (dark green) or there might be hazards to your health (muddy green).
Blue	This external color says that you are the situation and its resolution will impact your relationships. If the color is a dark rich blue, it means your relationships

will benefit as a result of you solving the situation. If the color is a muddy blue, it means that in solving the situation you may lose a relationship.

Purple   This external color is saying that somewhere in the process of resolving this situation you will be faced with a spiritual dilemma. If it is a muddy purple, the resolution of the problem may put you at odds with your ethics or beliefs. If it is a clear strong purple, then by resolving your situation you will be strengthening and honoring your ethics or beliefs.

Pink   This external color has to do with romance and love. Sometimes the color shows up when the situation being dealt with is currently affecting a romance. If the color is a muddy pink, then resolving the situation may cause problems in your romantic life. If the pink is clear, then resolving the situation will enhance or strengthen your romantic life. I remember one time when a pink background showed up surrounding silver and orange. The person was able to get a better job but this meant no longer working for their spouse's father. The fall out was problems with their spouse. I must say that they understood the translation of what they were seeing in the picture but they thought that would not happen, and were very surprise when it did.

Silver   The external factor here is finances, the marketplace, or economy. If the color is actually touching the wall or the hammer then you are picking up that your action or the situation is directly dependent on what is taking place in the economy.

Brown   The external factor expressed here is very interesting and not as common now as it used to be 20 years ago. This talks of the Status-quo. Brown surrounding the hammer or the wall is saying that resolving the situation will cause people to see you as a trouble maker or breaking some kind of code / tradition. I still see this sometimes when someone is trying to break through a "glass ceiling" type of situation. So, if you are set on resolving this situation, be aware that you may be criticized by your social circle or seen as "rocking the boat."

Life's Compass

DECISION MAKING / FINDING DIRECTION

If you have chosen the Life's Compass diagram for your exercise, you are working on finding or validating the direction that your life is taking or needs to take. You are interested in doing a check-point to see if your life is going according to your Life's Plan. This picture speaks to establishing a direction in life or it may be comparing where you are in reference to where you feel you need to be.

The first area to analyze is where you started to color. Did you first color the inner compass? This is a very important thing to understand about your situation because it talks of your focus today. If you started your picture with the inner compass, you are more concerned with where you are today. You want to validate if what you are doing in life is what you should be doing. If you colored the outer parts first, you are more concerned with where you life needs to be directed for the future. You are looking at the big picture of your life.

The second area to analyze is which point you colored first. If you colored the North point first, your inner-self is validating that you are on track. In this case your concerns might be with how to maintain this current track. If you colored the North point first, your inner-self is saying that your future direction is established and in synch with where you consciously want to go.

ONLY ONE COLOR ACROSS THE WHOLE PICTURE

This often indicates that there is one aspect of yourself dominating your whole outlook on life. You are having difficulty knowing whether your life is on track or not. The cause may be that this aspect has become so out of balance, maybe even out of control. Typically this happens with the colors described below. But, if the color you chose is not described below, then find where that color is discussed and apply that translation here using the same approach that is used below. Remember to also work the shade and stroke into your translation.

The color that you chose tells you what aspect is out of balance:

Red   Life is a challenge right now. Your emotions are on edge. You are feeling lost, fearful of the future, or frustrated by the obstacles in your way. Before you can address the direction of your life you need to address your emotions.

Suggested Action – give your body a way to express this pent up energy. Go for a walk, do some exercise, sing opera, or take a blank sheet of paper and fill it up with the strong bold strokes of red color. Now, that this energy has been vented, sit in a relaxed position and close your eyes. Take a slow deep breath and hold it for a few counts then slowly exhale. Repeat another two times. Breathing normally continue to sit in your relaxed position with your eyes closed. In your mind's eye see yourself sitting and surrounded by a soft white cool mist. Feel it refresh and calm you. Feel it heal your pain. With each inhale breathe in this refreshing, healing white mist. With each exhale breathe out the remaining red energy. After a few breaths you will notice that the red you are exhaling is softer and softer until it is more of a pink color. Thank your inner-self for communicating and working with you to bring back a balanced state. Count to three and open your eyes. Take a deep breath. You are done with the exercise.

Blue

The people in your life are influencing your choice of direction. These people are not necessarily people you love, since there is no pink. These are people you socialize with or work with. This is saying that you are at risk of falling into the stereotype of what your life should be because of who you associate with. Your inner-self is saying that you are allowing other people to make your life choices for you. The external voices are drowning out your internal voice. **Suggested Action** – This is a good time to review your life. Remember who you are. Remember what your dreams and hopes for yourself were as you were growing up and before you had been corrupted by your life's experiences. One way to do this is to do a meditation when you can be an observer of your own movie – a "This is your life" type of movie. Sit in a relaxed position and close your eyes. Take a slow deep breath and hold it for a few counts, then slowly exhale. Repeat another two times. Breathing normally, continue to sit in your relaxed position with your eyes closed. In your mind's eye see yourself watching a movie. Let the movie start at what ever age appears. Don't analyze at this point, just observe and acknowledge what you see and feel. Make a mental note of the times that you see yourself planning your future. If during the movie there are times when you see yourself talking about "when I grow up I want to…" make mental notes about that. Allow the movie to end naturally. Some people just see it stop and know that the flow of information is complete. Others say they suddenly see themselves sitting across from them; in other words the movie has caught up to where you are today. Yet, others see the movie go beyond today to where their inner-self feels they will be in the future. Thank your inner-self for this information. Take a deep breath, count to three and open your eyes. You are done with the meditation. While the memories of the meditation are fresh in your mind, write down your notes of what you saw, felt, and understood.

Keep these notes close to you over the next couple of days as you analyze and internalize what you saw. You will know when it is time to repeat the coloring exercise. Meanwhile, when the people around you make statements about your direction in life, mentally ask "what do I want to do?"

Green   Your concerns over health are blocking your insight into your future. These same concerns may even be interfering with your current life path. **Suggested Action** – You need to think about your perceptions about yourself and give them a reality check. If you feel you are not healthy, then go to the doctor. If you have been to the doctor and you checked out fine, but you can't let go of the feeling of being sick then you need to meditate on what is causing you to feel this way. If you are in good health but the stress is that your body does not look the way you think it should, then your meditation should focus on where these expectations came from and why. In addition to the meditation, you should also follow the below overall suggested action and go through that exercise every morning before starting your day until you feel your perceptions about your health are no longer blocking other information about your life.

OVERALL SUGGESTED ACTION

Now that you have addressed the energy that was blocking your view of life, do the exercise over. Pay attention to what is attracting to you to color first, and so on. Observe, don't analyze yet, just observe yourself coloring and acknowledge memories, thoughts, and ideas that surface while you are repeating the exercise. If you have removed the blocking energy, you may get a flood of ideas of where your life is going. Jot them down on the page so that you can explore them later, then continue with the coloring. If in the repeated exercise you again use only one color then work through it again, and again, until you start to see more colors. Sometimes there are layers of energy that need to be cleared before being able to get a more complete picture.

If after a couple of times of repeating the exercise you find yourself still only using the same color, then you need to pause. Try again another day. It could be that current events are so overwhelming that you need to take a moment to relax. If you are still feeling like you need to color, but can't get beyond the one color with this diagram, then work with another diagram. I have found that the Candlelight and the Lotus Flower both are helpful in breaking through the blocking energy. They help you focus on the higher-self, or greater meaning of life. In a way they help you look beyond the problems that are facing you today and bring back hope that there is better life beyond your present tribulation.

OUTER SECTIONS AND COLORS

In general, this diagram can be analyzed in three sections; past, present, and future. The Western coordinates speak to aspects of your past that are acting on your current path or the path that you are leading to in the future. The eastern coordinates speak of the aspects that you need to work on as you progress in time. So, the left of the page is what you are working on from your past. The right of the page is what you see yourself working on in the future. These are aspects of yourself that influence and are important to your life's direction now and in the future. The middle of the diagram speaks to your current path and the path you are heading toward in your future. Notice that this section of the diagram speaks to the path itself, not about you. Sometimes the South point is the one that stands out, this means that you are still transitioning from one path to another. In other words, you are completing one cycle or chapter of your life and starting another.

Western points The western points speak to the aspects of yourself that are acting on you today. What about yourself is influencing some of the decisions you need to make about your path.

Red	in general, red speaks of emotions. If the red is clear, the emotion is more of a passion like a belief in a cause. If the red is darker with brown in it, more like a brick color, then the emotion is that of anger, frustration, fear, or anxiety. This is saying that your emotions in the past drove your decisions. Is that what you want to continue to do? This is a time to reassess how you make life decisions. Maybe the only way you got to where you are is through your passion or anger. But, is this the way you want to continue? The statement here is that this is the time to have this internal dialogue. If you see the red extend to more sections as you move toward the east, you are reacting to life rather than being in control of your life. It is time to get emotions under control.
Orange	this color speaks to the survival level; things like job, finances, and home. This means that you have faced challenges in the survival level in the past. Perhaps lost your job or lost your house? Whatever challenges in the survival level you have overcome are now influencing your decisions about moving forward. You need to ask yourself whether you are making decisions about where you want to go in life, or are you making decision out of fear of falling on hard times again? You need to analyze why you fell on hard times and release these fears, or else you could be cheating yourself out of a much better future.
Yellow	This color says that you have used your intelligence in the past to get to where you are today. A clear bright yellow means that your ability to gather information and put it to good use in your life is an ability that you still have and will continue to use. If the color is muddy then it is says that you have not made very intelligent choices in the past and it is a warning to be smarter about things going forward.

| Green | This color often shows up in this diagram when someone feels that their state of health is what influenced the path to where they are today. So, a dark green says that you feel your good health was an integral part of getting to where you are today. A yellowish or muddy green says that you are where you are today as a result of bad health. Either way, green says that health was a strong influence on how and why you are where you are. |

| Blue | This color says that in the past you have based your decisions on what other people say or think. You were influenced by others' expectations and judgments. This is the time to reassess and decide if you still believe in them or as they do. This a good time to find out who you really are, as opposed to who you have been trying to be. |

| Purple | This color says that your beliefs, ethics, and spirituality have played an important part in how you made your decisions. If the color is clear and strong, your spirituality has supported you and given you the foundation you needed to get here. It is an aspect of yourself that you can continue to count on for support and strength. If the color is muddy, it is saying that somewhere along the way you compromised or betrayed your ethics. You Spiritual self is reminding you of what you did to get to where you are and asking to be revisited. |

| Pink | This color is saying that love was a great source of inspiration for your decision making. Love is where your strength has been and it is greatly responsible for getting you to where you are today. This is an aspect of yourself that will continue to support you and strengthen your resolve of getting to where you want to go. A muddy pink speaks about a love situation that led you astray. You feel that you made decisions for love that you wouldn't have otherwise made. More internal dialogue is necessary here. Love is supposed to be a positive influence. If it was not, then maybe you mistook something else for love. This might be a warning to look deeper into a situation and don't be too quick to assume that someone is advising you out of love or with love. |

| Silver | This color speaks to the financial situation that you are reacting to. Something about money, making it or losing it, has influenced your decisions in the past. Money was your guide and your inspiration. You need to reassess. Do you still want money to be your drive? Because right now it still is strongly influencing your decisions. |

| Brown | This color speaks to the amount of discipline you have shown in the past. If it is a dark and clear brown, it speaks of how your discipline has helped you get to where you are today. If it is a muddy or messy brown, then it says that you have lacked discipline in the past and warns of this lack of discipline being an obstacle to your future. |

Black	This color is saying that you don't want to remember where you came from. You are trying to be someone different. Are you ashamed of who you were or where you came from? You are hiding something about your past and this effort is interfering with the decisions you will need to make. Is hiding this past limiting what you want to do or where you want to go? Would it be easier to face your past and be free from it rather than be a slave to its continual denial? You may think that you are hiding from it but it will catch up with you unless you address it once and for all.

Eastern points This section of the diagram speaks to aspects of yourself that will help you going forward or will present challenges for you. By raising your awareness of these aspects, you inner-self is giving you a chance to better position yourself for success.

Red	If this color is a clear red, your passion and strong emotional belief in what you are doing will get you there. This is saying that in order to be successful you need to be passionate about what you are doing. If this color is a muddy color, it is saying to beware, because your emotions will trip you up. You emotions will create situations that will work against you. Now is the time to learn to get your emotions under control.
Orange	This color is saying that in the future your concern for the survival level will be driving your decisions. If the color is clear, it says that you will be able to maintain a positive survival level and use it as a spring board or stepping stone. If the color is muddy, it says that your fear of having problems in the survival level will tend to limit your risk taking. You will tend to make decisions based on your fear of not being able to take care of the survival level. You are still too focused on the day-to-day to be able to see where your life is leading.
Yellow	This color speaks to knowledge and information. Take the time to do your due diligence. This is definitely a sign to plan each step carefully. Rely on your intelligence to make the right decision. If the color is a muddy yellow, be aware that someone might be putting out misinformation. Sometimes, this is seen in situations where someone is planting information or misrepresenting a situation. Muddy yellow means that you need to verify every piece of information before making a decision.
Green	This color is saying that going forward you need to focus more on your health. You might be sensing that the pace you have been keeping or the sacrifices you have been making will catch up with you. This is the time to prevent bad health.
Blue	This color says that people will be an influence on your decisions. If the color is a clear blue, it states that your personal network will be of help to you on your way to the top. You should start working on building a strong network now. If the color is a muddy blue, you will have a tendency to want to please

others more than yourself. Your decisions on what direction to take your life will be more based on what others expect of you than what you want for yourself.

Purple   This situation includes an ethics aspect. This color is saying that you might encounter a conflict of ethics or beliefs when planning your future. If purple was in your past, your spiritual self seems to be a life's lesson. You could be saying that you are going to prove that you can make it to the top without losing your spirituality. If the color is muddy, you will be tempted to betray your beliefs and ethics in exchange for success.

Pink   A clear strong pink says that love will be your guide and strength in making key life decisions. A muddy pink says that you need to be careful with love relationships because you will have a tendency to be led astray by someone professing love. Take a look at the bigger picture and verify that the decision is right from other aspects as well, not just from the view of love.

Silver   Money will be a strong driver in your decision making. If the color is clear, you are headed toward some good opportunities for financial success. If the color is muddy or dirty, you are going to be tempted to "sell out", or betray yourself for money.

Brown   This color says that discipline will play a key factor in your decision making. If the color is dark and clear, you need to keep discipline to position yourself for success. If the color is dirty or murky, it says that your lack of discipline will be your undoing.

Black   This color says that you are trying not to have any pre-conceived ideas of what your future may be. You are trying to stay open to whatever comes. But, if this was really true, then why did you select this diagram to work with. Are you being honest with yourself? Or, are you afraid to place expectations on yourself for fear of letting yourself down? You need to have an internal dialogue around this.

Northern point Based on where you are today, this is where you will end up. This might be where you will reach your peak, or your ultimate success. It may speak of where your next cycle or chapter of life will take you. When you selected this diagram you must have had a question or idea of what the future would hold. Use your definition of the future to tell you what this northern point is talking about.

Red   This color is saying if you continue as you are going you will end up in a state of strong emotions. If the color is clear, you are headed to a point in life where you will be dedicating your life to a cause. Something that you believe in so strongly that you will dedicate your life to making this cause a success. If the color is muddy, you are heading down a path that will lead to emotional turmoil. Deal with your emotions now or they will become much more difficult to deal with as they will continue to compound.

Orange   This color says that your future will be focused around the survival level. You are more interested in making sure you have a roof over your head and food on the table than you are of accomplishing some grand thing in life. Look at the other areas of the picture. Are there some clues as to why you are limiting your future to just the survival level? Is there some fears that are stopping you from aspiring to something more?

Yellow   This says that your future will entail working with knowledge. Either your claim to fame and glory will be something you invent or something you become an expert at. Your future will be focused on using your intelligence; this might be teaching, inventing, studying, writing, or any field that requires a great deal of intelligence and focus of thought.

Green   Your future will be very involved with the area of health. If the color is a bright dark green, it says you will be working in the health field. Your focus will be helping others achieve health. If the color is a muddy green, it speaks about your health suffering based on what you are doing today. This is a warning to change what you are doing today so that you can save your health.

Blue   Your future will be focused on dealing with people. If this is a clear blue, you will be working with people. You may be a counselor, therapist, or consultant; any field where you are working directly with people and advising them on their decisions and direction. If this is a muddy blue, then your future will be dealing with difficult people situations.

Purple   Your future will be focused on spirituality. You may become a spiritual leader. Or, you may focus on developing your psychic abilities. The overall statement is that your life will be dedicated to enhancing your spiritual nature and using it to help others.

Pink   This color says that love is in your future. Your life will be focused on experiencing love and living in love.

Silver   This color speaks to your financial future. If the color is clear, you will have a strong financial future or that you will be working in the finance field. If the color is muddy, it says that you will be dealing with financial issues. This can be yourself in dealing with your own financial troubles or it can be working in a field where you are helping people that are having financial problems.

Southern point This is an interesting section of the picture. It talks to what might happen if you don't move forward. So this talks of the consequences of not working on what you need to work on. You can call it a backslide, or it may be an alternate future based on the decisions you are making. The color translations are the same as for the Northern point.

Inner Circle These colors speak to what is acting on you today as you make your decisions about your future. They can be the obstacles that are stopping you from progressing toward your future plans. Or, they can be the aspects of yourself that you need to rely on to press forward. I have found that usually the inner compass is all one color. But, if you have more than one color in the inner compass then you are having more than one aspect to work on or work with. So, treat them as equally important.

Red   If this is a clear red, it is saying that your emotional drive, and your passion, is what will get you to the next step toward your future plans. If the color is a muddy red, it is saying that what is stopping you from progressing is your emotions; anger, fear, anxiety, and the like. If you don't address these emotions then you can look to the southern point to show you what you are heading toward instead of the future you planned.

Orange   Your concern for your future is keeping you in place. You are comfortable where you are and you don't have any compelling reason to move forward. You are mainly focused on keeping a roof over your head and food on your plate. If you don't find something to work towards then look at what you have drawn in the southern point to see where you will end up in the future.

Yellow   If this is a clear color, it is saying that your intelligence is your key to your future. This can mean your education, your ability to find and use information, and your ability to make smart decisions. If the color is a muddy yellow, it is saying that what is holding you back from your planned future is your lack of intelligence in making decisions. You need to learn to look at a situation from all angles and make sure you have enough information to make decisions. Making decisions without enough information is what is holding you back from your future plans.

Green   This color is saying that your state of health is playing an important role in your progress toward the future. If the color is clear, your strong health will help you get to where you want to be. If the color is muddy, you need to get your health in order before you tackle your future plans.

Blue   If this is a clear color, you are working on your network and it is this network of people that will help you get to where you are going. If the color is muddy, your obstacle is that you are listening to the wrong people. You are making decisions based on what others are saying and expecting of you, rather than based on what you want and know. You need to trust yourself more. And above all else, you need to know yourself better before proceeding.

Purple   This color is saying that your spirituality is the doorway to your future. Keep your faith strong. Stick to your ethics and beliefs for they will get you there.

Pink	This color is saying that much of what you will accomplish you will do with love and for love. If the color is clear, love is your strength and it will get you there. If the color is muddy, confusion about love is getting in the way of making the right decisions, as they pertain to your future.
Silver	This is saying that money is what will get you to where you are going. This might speak of an investment you need to make in order to achieve your goals. Or, it may mean that you need to manage your money better in order to make progress toward your future.
Brown	This color is saying that your level of discipline is your doorway to the future. If the color is clear and dark, your strong discipline and will power will help you succeed. If the color is muddy, your lack of discipline in stopping you from moving forward.
Black	This color is saying that there are some unknowns that are influencing your future. Take each step with as many safety precautions as you can think of, because there is something or someone who is influencing your future and at this point you don't know if this is a good thing or a bad thing.

Tree of Life

WORKING ON STRENGTH, GROWTH, COURAGE

The selection of this diagram says that you are working on yourself. You feel that before moving forward with other aspects of your life you need to enhance your own inner strength. This is a time in your life to assess what you have accomplished and give yourself a pat on the back. This is also a time to say that although the path has been tough you want to continue on. You are ready to work on some of your karmic lessons. You are ready to prepare to face your inner feelings. You are no longer afraid of admitting that you have shortcomings, because you are ready to address them. All in all you are ready to become the next evolution of yourself in this life. You should recognize that by selecting this diagram you are expressing courage and belief in your own strength to grow.

The first area to analyze is where you started to color. Was your first color on the roots, the trunk, or the tree top? Where you start speaks of how you are going about developing your inner strength. It talks to your approach toward growth.

TREE ROOTS AS THE STARTING POINT

This starting point indicates that you are looking to your heritage, your background, your family, and your past for your strength. You feel that by seeing the greatness in these areas you will feel inspired to grow and have courage to tackle the future. Or, you might feel that by reviewing your past and addressing the pain and turmoil that you have endured, you will be released from your past and allowed to grow. You understand that it takes courage and strength to face your past, but you are ready.

TREE TRUNK AS THE STARTING POINT

This starting point indicates that you are at peace with your past and feel that it is more important right now to focus on what is driving you to grow. You want to understand what is supporting your growth, you driving force, your basis for strength.

TREE TOP AS THE STARTING POINT

This starting point says that your focus is your growth today and going forward. You feel adequately supported and have made peace with your past. You feel that understanding your inspiration and potential is what is important in your life today.

YOU ADDED FRUIT TO THE PICTURE

This is very interesting because you are saying that you want to achieve this growth for more than just yourself. You want to feel that there will be tangible benefits to your growth. You have certain expectations of how inner growth will benefit you and those around you. Look to the color translation guide to help you understand what these expectations are.

The second thing to analyze about your picture is the colors you used in the picture. Remember to also take the shade and strokes into consideration when translating your colors. The shade and stroke are discussed in the preface of this section.

ONLY ONE COLOR ACROSS THE WHOLE PICTURE

This often indicates that there is one aspect of yourself that you feel is in your way of growth. This must be a difficult aspect for you to face to have gone so long without addressing it, thus by addressing it today you are also working on your courage and strength. What is this aspect that so has you concerned?

The color that you chose speaks to what aspect you want to work on as your first step toward growth:

Red	The aspect of yourself that you need to work on is your emotional self. Your emotions are ruling your reactions to life and your decision-making. This is the first place to begin your journey toward growth, strength of character, and wisdom.
	Suggested Action – make a conscious effort to analyze your reactions before responding to a situation. In arguments, don't take everything that is said as a personal rejection. Detach yourself from what is being said and focus more on why the person is saying these things. By understanding the "why" you will be able to have more compassion and patience toward the other person. What follows is being able to stop taking everything that is said personally. The eventual goal is to be able to focus on how to resolve the issues rather than worrying about how to win the argument.
Blue	Your focus on interpersonal relationships is distracting you from your own journey. There needs to be clearer boundaries between you and others. The question you need to ask yourself is "Am I using the excuse of helping others

as a way to not focus on myself?" This can become a habit. When helping others through their problems, you feel good about yourself. Yes, you did a good deed, but unless you learned from it, you didn't make any progress in your own growth. Continually focusing on the faults and problems of others is a way to deny that we ourselves have faults and problems. Also, when we become chronic helpers we encourage those we help to become dependent on us. This starts a downward spiritual spiral for both parties. Sometimes the way to help is to let the other person take care of their own problems.

Suggested Action – Make a conscious effort to think about what is being asked of you before responding. When someone asks for help, ask yourself a series of questions. Are they really asking for help or are you just assuming that they need help and volunteering or pushing your assistance on them? Sometimes people just want someone to listen to them and that in itself is the help that they need. Is the person asking for help someone who has become lazy? Are they used to everyone else taking care of them and therefore they don't have to take responsibility for their own life? By helping these types of friends and relatives you are stopping them from growing up into responsible people. Often these people will use emotional guilt trips to convince you to help them. "You are the only one that has ever helped me." "You know how hard I've had it, I just need a few bucks to make it through the next few days." Look deeper into their request. Are they in this predicament because they made bad choices? For example, is this person in need of some cash because they went out partying with the rent money? Or, do they need a place to stay for a few months because they spent their money on a new car or expensive vacations, and now don't have enough money to pay the rent? By helping this person you are telling them that it is acceptable for them to not take responsibility for themselves. Make it a conscious effort to think about what you are doing before agreeing to help. In general having blue as the only color on this picture is saying that the type of relationships you have established are providing you with the spiritual lessons and problems that you need to overcome in order to continue on your path to higher self.

Green   The current lesson that you are faced with deals with the physical body and health. If the color is deep and rich, your lesson is to overcome these health issues through taking control of your life. The lesson is to focus all your aspects on achieving good health. That is use your spiritual self, your intelligence, your passion and love of life, your discipline, and your love for yourself to overcome the challenges facing you in this area. If the color is a yellowish or muddy green, you need help in the area of health. You may be in denial and it is time to admit that there is a problem. It is this denial that is holding you back from progressing on your spiritual path toward growth. **Suggested Action** – you need to think about your perceptions about yourself and give them a reality check. If you feel you are not healthy, go to the doctor. If you have been to the doctor and you checked out fine, but you can't let go of the feeling of being sick then you need to meditate on what is causing you to feel this way. If you are in good health but the stress is that your body does not look the way you think it should, then your meditation should focus on where these expectations came from and why. In addition to the meditation, you should also follow the below overall suggested action and go through that exercise every morning before starting your day until you feel your perceptions about your health and or body are back in balance with the rest of your life.

Yellow   The current lesson is to have a healthier balance between intelligence and intuition. This may mean that you are trying to solve everything through logic and not taking the human, emotional, love, or spiritual aspects of situations into considerations. The other interpretation is that you may be denying your intelligent side. You are dealing with life in a reactive mode and need to start thinking about your actions and decisions more.

OVERALL SUGGESTED ACTION

Meditate on the color you have used and try to apply the translation to your own life. Review your past as the memories come to the surface. Are you dealing with patterns in your lives that are stopping you from growing? Focus on this color for a few days and then go through the exercise again. See if the color changes. If it is still one color and the same, then continue to work through it until the exercise yields a different color.

SECTIONS AND COLORS

Tree roots These colors speak to your past, your family, and your foundation. In some cases you will be expressing a positive aspect about your foundation. The color is indicating what aspect of yourself to access from your past to sustain you through the current tribulations. Other times, the color is indicating an area of your past that needs to be healed or resolved as a way to move forward on your life's path. Look to other aspect of the color as a way to distinguish between the type of influences that the past has on your current growth. These other aspects were spoken in the preface of this section. They are the stroke and shade of the color, the area of the page that you colored first, whether the color is alone or in combination with another color. All of these aspects can help you be more specific in your translation of the message.

Red   Red in the roots says that there are some negative emotions from the past that you need to resolve in order to progress on your path. This may be anger toward someone, a traumatic experience, a pattern of painful experiences that have predisposed you to certain personality traits. There needs to be some healing of the past. The fact that you selected this picture and these colors says that you are ready to forgive and be forgiven. You are ready to move on and let the past rest in peace. This is a time for lots of meditation. Maybe even a time to find a counselor to talk with about these things. Your first step is to recognize how far you have come since then and acknowledge that you have already overcome some of the past's hold on you. It is a matter of completing the process.

Orange
How your survival was taken care of in your growing up years is still so engrained that it is strongly influencing your reactions in your present life. You need to take the time to educate yourself to the fact that the conditions and situations that your family was in back then is not the same as the ones that you are experiencing right now. You need to let go of the fears and habits of that time. This can go in either direction. For example, if you were brought up in a very affluent environment but now you don't have a lot of money but are having difficulties staying within budget. You are angry because you don't understand why you don't have more money. You need to go over the decisions and events that have happened to change your situation and change your attitudes accordingly. Another example, if you grew up in a family that didn't have much but today you earn a very good income. Yet, you can't bring yourself to spend money or are always buying the cheapest things for yourself and others. A part of you is still afraid that you may end up like your parents and find yourself with not enough money. This fear is holding you back from making decisions that are more appropriate for your life today.

Yellow
There is important information in your past. It would benefit you to review the past and learn from it. It is this information that will help you in your path toward growth. If the yellow is a muddy color, then be aware that the information you uncover may not be what you think. There may be some truths that were covered up and it is now time to uncover them.

Green
How health was dealt with in your growing up years is very much dictating how you deal with health today. For example, did a key person in your life use their poor health to manipulate other family members? If so, do you find yourself getting sick often and usually it is around a situation you don't want to deal with? Another thing I have seen, is when as a youngster you did not receive compassion or nurturing when you were ill. Now, you find it hard to have patience or compassion for your loved ones when they are ill. As a matter of fact it makes you angry to see them ill. It is time to review the attitudes toward health in your past and adjust your attitudes based on this information.

Blue
It is the people from your past that will sustain you through the dark periods. This color in the roots says that you have strong relationships or a strong network of friends and family that you can count on. If the color is muddy, then it states the opposite. It says that help from these people in the past

comes with strings attached. These relationships are important or they would not have shown up. So, your task is to review these relationships and establish your understanding of what you can and can not count on them for. This will make the path going forward much more pleasant.

Purple   This color is saying that your spirituality is the foundation and key to your strength, courage, and growth. Keep your faith strong. Stick to your ethics and beliefs for they will get you there. If the color is muddy, it says that the interpretation of the spiritual beliefs held by your family needs to be revisited. There may be some erroneous interpretations that you need to be aware of. You need to revisit your own beliefs and see if some of them need to be adjusted to this new information.

Pink   If the color is clear, it is saying that love is your strength and it will get you there. If the color is muddy, it is saying that your confusion about love is getting in the way of making the right decisions, as they pertain to your future. Either way, pink in the roots is saying that love is a strong influence in your life. The shade and stroke of this color in the roots may shed light on how you deal with love in your life today.

Tree trunk These colors deal with what is supporting your path today. These colors can talk about your current career or current relationships. These are the influencing elements that will get you to your goals or are the obstacles on your path.

Red   If this is a clear red, it is saying that your emotional drive, your passion, is what will get you to the next step toward your future. If the color is a muddy red, it is saying that what is stopping you from progressing is your emotions; anger, fear, anxiety, and the like. You need to learn to manage your emotions better so that they don't rule your decisions and reactions in life.

Orange   Your concern for your future is keeping you in place. You are comfortable where you are and you don't have any compelling reason to move forward. You are mainly focused on keeping a roof over your head and food on your plate. If the tree top is something other than orange then you are not in synch with yourself. You might have unrealistic expectations or are not willing to take the risks necessary to go after your dreams.

Yellow   If this is a clear color, it is saying that your intelligence is your key to your future. This can mean your education, your ability to find and use information, and your ability to make smart decisions. If the color is a muddy yellow, it is saying that what is holding you back from your planned future is your lack of intelligence in making decisions. You need to learn to look at a situation from all angles and make sure you have enough information to make decisions. Making decisions without enough information is what is holding you up from your future plans.

Green	This color is saying that your state of health is playing an important role in your progress toward the future. If the color is clear, your strong health will help you get to where you want to be. If the color is muddy, you need to get your health in order before you tackle your future plans.
Blue	If this is a clear color, you are working on your network and it is this network of people that will help you get to where you are going. If the color is muddy, your obstacle is that you are listening to the wrong people. You are making decisions based on what others are saying and expecting of you rather than based on what you want and know. You need to trust yourself more. And above all else, you need to know yourself better before proceeding.
Purple	This color is saying that your spirituality is the doorway to your future. Keep your faith strong. Stick to your ethics and beliefs for they will get you there.
Pink	This color is saying that much of what you will accomplish you will do with love and for love. If the color is clear, it is saying that love is your strength and it will get you there. If the color is muddy, it is saying that your confusion about love is getting in the way of making the right decisions, as they pertain to your future.
Silver	This is saying that money is what will get you to where you are going. This might speak of an investment you need to make in order to achieve your goals. Or, it might say that you need to manage your money better in order to make progress toward your future.
Brown	This color is saying that your level of discipline is your doorway to the future. If the color is clear and dark, it speaks of your strong discipline and will power as the source of your success. If the color is muddy, it is saying that your lack of discipline is stopping you from moving forward.

Tree top These colors talk of what you are heading toward. What your growth will translate into. What you will reach if you have the strength and courage to face the challenges and learn the lessons.

Red	Red tree tops tend to speak of finding a cause that you will become passionate about. It is speaking of strong emotions; usually these are at the positive end of the emotional spectrum.
Orange	This is the color of the physical level and survival. When the tree top has orange, it is a statement that the survival level will be taken care of. It is an encouragement that the risk is worth taking.
Yellow	This is saying that your growth will bring with it enlightenment and a higher intelligence.

Green	Sometimes a green tree top speaks of achieving good health through growth of spirit. Other times it says that your spiritual path will find you in the healing field. You will become a healer of sorts.
Blue	Your growth will take you into a position or career where you will be working with people. Helping people will be your way of life.
Purple	This color as a tree top speaks of a spiritual calling. This means that your path toward growth will translate into a calling to work in the spiritual field.
Pink	Once you overcome the lessons and challenges you are faced with today, you will find love. What you are working through today is what is holding you back from Love.
Silver	There is a financial reward at the end of your journey. Overcoming your challenges and obstacles today will translate into a financial reward.

Added fruit Adding fruit to your picture says that you are very focused on the "fruits of your labor." You need to check your reasons and attitudes. The path toward growth should not have these strings attached. Spiritual growth is not something to negotiate. The fact that you have grown in courage and strength should be its own reward.

Red	You believe that by overcoming the challenges of today's life you will be able to get back at the people who have made you suffer. The red fruit signifies revenge. You need to work on forgiveness. This red fruit will end up spoiling your success.
Orange	Your concern for the survival level will not go away completely when you reach your goals. They will come back and haunt you. It is better to address these concerns of the survival level before you move forward so that they don't spoil your success or maybe even sabotage your success.
Yellow	Part of reaching your future self will mean becoming enlightened. The yellow fruit is aspects of enlightenment that will break through as you overcome the challenges you are facing.
Green	An added reward to your reaching your future self will be good health.
Blue	Your aspirations of reaching the "in-crowd" are showing through. You feel that if you can grow you can be accepted into the type of social circle that you want to belong to. This can become a circular argument because as you grow you care less about "fitting in" and often this makes you more appealing to others which in turn means that you will be more accepted, but by then you won't really care if you are "accepted". It is funny how this works out.
Purple	Purple fruit is saying that part of your reward for growth is becoming more spiritual and sharing that spirituality.

Pink   Your reason for wanting to grow is that you feel that by overcoming or learning the lessons facing you, you will be more worthy of love. Similar to the Blue, this can become a circular argument, but it is a benefit none the less. You will have love as a result of growth, but only because you will feel worthy of it and allow yourself to be loved.

Silver   Your hopes are that courage, strength, and personal growth will bring with it financial rewards. Silver fruit does mean that there will be some financial rewards, but the fact that they are fruit and not the whole tree top means that these will be in scattered events. Again, don't put these expectations on your growth because the expectations themselves will sabotage their manifestation.

Sunrise / Sunset

WORKING ON STABILITY, MATURITY, FAMILY

If you have chosen the Sunrise / Sunset diagram for your exercise this says that you are feeling the need for a more stable and predictable environment. Your life has had so many twists and turns that you need to take a rest. Your life may have been very exciting and enjoyable but your spirit is now asking for peace. No, you are not getting old, you are just growing up.

The symbolism of this picture is that no matter how bad things get, or how tired you are, there is always tomorrow. Tomorrow might hold another chance to do things right. Tomorrow might hold better opportunities. Your choice in this diagram says that although you might be tired from the battles you have been faced with, you are not ready to give up.

The first area to analyze is where you started to color. Was your first color the sun, the mountain, the foothills, or the river? Where you start speaks of what your spirit is asking for in order to feel safe, stable, nurtured.

RIVER AS THE STARTING POINT

This starting point indicates that you are looking for cleansing. You may be feeling that you have gotten yourself into a situation that there is no way out of. You want a chance to start over with a clean slate. Is your past catching up with you? Have you been spending too much time covering up the past or trying to escape it? This cleansing of the soul can happen, but it won't be easy. You need to meditate on how to forgive others, forgive yourself, and asking forgiveness from those who got hurt in the process.

FOOTHILLS AS THE STARTING POINT

You feel you have made much progress toward the stable and happy life that you are searching for. However, you also feel that there are some major challenges coming up that will interfere with you reaching your promised land. You might ask yourself what evidence you have that these challenges exist? Or is it that you believe that you have to experience hardship before you can be worthy of the good life? These upcoming tribulations might be in your mind, and you might be working to make them self-fulfilling prophecies. Meditate on the topic of being worthy of a happy and stable life.

MOUNTAIN AS THE STARTING POINT

Your soul is feeling strong, stable, and satisfied. You feel that your life has been worth while. You want to leave some sort of legacy of wisdom to those you love. But, don't start thinking that you are done. There is still fire left in you. There is still much for you to enjoy, so remind yourself that this is only a pause or check-point before continuing on to the next adventure.

SUN AS THE STARTING POINT

Your focus is on the outcome. Regardless of what stage of your journey you are in, you want to know what the pot at the end of the rainbow holds for you.

Now ask yourself whether you colored a sunrise or a sunset? If you colored a sunrise, you are hopeful and positive; an optimist. You are ready to tackle the world and reach your goal.

If you colored a sunset, you are tired and need a pause before continuing forward. You feel you are toward the end of the journey but are not sure if you have what it takes to make the home stretch. Remember that our life's agenda has allowed for all of the twists and turns and pauses we would take. So, don't give in to that sense of urgency that you are feeling. There is enough time for the rest that you need and you will make it to the "Promised Land" with plenty of time to enjoy it.

ONLY ONE COLOR ACROSS THE WHOLE PICTURE

Your inner-self is telling you that this main aspect – as represented by the color – is what stands between you and the life you seek. Stability, maturity, peace, and nurturing are on the other side of this major lesson that you need to work through.

The color that you chose tells you what this major lesson is:

Red Your emotions are not letting you see clearly. You may have already accomplished what you seek but you don't see it because you have so much emotion in the way. For a daily exercise you can follow the suggested action. In addition, this is the time for you to learn emotion management techniques. These may be talking with a counselor, joining a support group, or taking a class in meditation, Tai Chi, or Yoga. The objective is to be able to calm yourself enough so that you can look beyond the immediate emotions. **Suggested Action** – give your body a way to express this pent up emotion. Go for a walk, do some exercise, sing opera, or take a blank sheet of paper and fill it up with the strong bold strokes of red color. Now that this energy has been vented, sit in a relaxed position and close your eyes. Take a slow deep breath and hold it for a few counts, then slowly exhale. Repeat another two times. Breathing normally continue to sit in your relaxed position with your eyes closed. In your mind's eye see yourself sitting and surrounded by a soft white cool mist. Feel it refresh and calm you. Feel it heal your pain. With each inhale breathe in this refreshing, healing white mist. With each exhale breathe out the remaining red energy. After a few breaths, you will notice that the red you are exhaling is softer and softer until it is more of a pink color. Thank your inner-self for communicating and working with you to bring back a balanced state. Count to three and open your eyes. Take a deep breath. You are done with the exercise.

Blue

The lesson facing you is that of knowing which people to include in your life. You may have "hanger-oners"; these are people that you have kept in your life out of habit or because you just don't know how to get rid of them. These people are like leeches. They are taking your spiritual energy and leaving you too tired to continue on your path. Analyze your circle of friends, family, and business acquaintances. You know which ones you don't need or want in your life anymore. Make a plan for how to bring a peaceful and loving closure to those relationships. This is not a time for confrontation. This is a time for peaceful good byes.

Green

You have concerns about your health or you physical being. If the shade of green is a yellowish green then you are concerned about illness or fearful that you will become ill. If the shade of green is a dark green, you are too focused on your physical self almost to the exclusion of other aspects of your life. Sometimes this happens when people become obsessed with their body and become addicted to exercise or diets. Essentially your source of stress is that your body is not what you want it to be and feel that you are failing in some way because of it. Another way to think of this is that you are holding yourself back from the stable life that you seek. You are holding yourself back because you are afraid that you will stagnate or become bored. You are afraid of the physical consequences of changing your life. You are forgetting that you are the one in control and this new life you seek is what you define it to be. Having stability, maturity, and nurturing in your life does not have to exclude excitement, activity, or fun.

Silver

You are concerned that reaching for this stable and nurturing life is going to create financial problems for you. Maybe this is a time to do financial planning so that you have a better idea of what you have to work with and minimize the unknowns. This life you seek does not need to exclude aspects of your current life that you enjoy. You can have a stable and nurturing life and still have a career that earns the level of income you enjoy. You need to do more planning of what this life you seek is. Think of the details. Think of what you truly need, don't just assume that everything you have now has to stay the same. It is up to you to design this new life.

OVERALL SUGGESTED ACTION

As a way to start to welcome the life you seek, repeat the exercise. This time make it a purposeful coloring. Color the picture the way you would like to see it. Make it the prettiest you can. Color it in such a way that you enjoy looking at it. Looking at it should make you feel warm, peaceful, and happy. It may take several tries, but keep working at it until you get it just right. Fine tune the colors until you get the desired emotional effects when you look at it. Now, frame it and put in somewhere where you can see it every day. When you feel tired or frustrated or stressed with life, look at your picture. Let it ease your concerns. Let it remind you of what you are working towards.

SECTIONS AND COLORS

River The color you used on the river speaks of what you need cleansed in your life. This is what is dragging you down. By cleansing this aspect of your life you can then turn the river into a soothing, refreshing source of energy.

Red
You need to cleanse your emotions. You have too much anger, pain, or frustration. Follow the exercise for releasing red energy. Follow this exercise every morning and evening so that you can bring this aspect of yourself into balance with what you want your life to be.

Orange
You need to cleanse your attitude about the survival level and physical aspect of your life. You are hyperactive and need to find a more positive way to express this energy. Your energy is a bit scattered, you don't follow through on projects you set for yourself. You keep very busy but it is not always the type of busy that is good or needed. **Suggested Action** - plan and follow-through on projects that make your environment healthier, beautiful, and more valuable. This is the time to fix your house, work in your garden, clean out your closets. It is time that you stop worrying about your survival level and actually start doing something about it. Start making your surroundings more pleasant to live in.

Yellow
You need to stop this "analysis paralysis." It is good to analyze and be logical when it comes to the business and financial aspects of your life. But, you take this too far. You analyze everything in your life to the point of getting lost in meaningless detail. Learn to bring intelligence and intuition in balance. Take a class in meditation, Tai Chi, or Yoga. Take an art class. Open up your creative center so that you can see what this aspect of yourself has to offer in your life.

Green
You need to cleanse your body. There are some habits that are hurting your body and your chances for a better life. This is the time to stop doing drugs, stop smoking, or stop drinking. Take a look at your habits and develop a plan of attack. Get some help. Your body needs to be cleansed.

Blue
It is time to cleanse your relationships. This is the time to let go of those

relationships which are no longer in synch with who you are or want to be. These relationships are dragging you down.

Purple	It is time to cleanse your spiritual beliefs. This means that you may have inherited your belief system and have ended up with a set of beliefs that you follow out of habit but not because you truly believe in them. Think about your spiritual nature and take your spiritual beliefs seriously. Are you just going through the motions? Be conscious of what you believe in and what that belief means as far as ethics and behavior.
Silver	Your attachment to money needs to be cleared. Being so focused on money is dragging other aspects of your life down. Bring it back in balance. Take a look at what it is costing you to be so attached to money. Do you really want to sacrifice all other aspects of your life for money?
Brown	Your strictness to a particular discipline is holding you back from reaching a state of happiness. Are you so strict that you don't allow for any excitement or fun in your life? Or do you lack so much discipline that you never get anything done on time? Either extreme can interfere with reaching the stable, happy, nurturing life you seek.
Sparkles	This is one of the few diagrams where I tend to see sparkles show up. If you put sparkles in your river, it says that you need to come back to reality. Your expectations of the life you seek is not realistic. You have confused your dreams with your goals. Take a look at what you are searching for and make sure it really is what you want and not just a fantasy.

Foothills This area of the picture speaks to the valley you find yourself in right now in your life. You have anticipation or expectation of some "spiritual test" or challenge coming up that will make you worthy of the life you seek. The question you should ask yourself is "without this test or challenge would I still feel worthy of the life I want?" This is very important. Because you may be closer than you think to reaching your goal. But, if you want a challenge, you will create this challenge for yourself, just to make you feel worthy.

Red	You are working on building up your passion for your goal. You are getting yourself emotionally ready to tackle what is coming and ready to accept the rewards. Just be careful not to build up this readiness for battle so much that when you reach your goal it is anti-climatic. Focus more on what you want to achieve and not so much on how hard it will be to get it.
Orange	You feel that currently you are just taking care of the day-to-day as you wait for that golden opportunity. Are you sure that the opportunity is coming to you and not the other way around. You need to be more proactive in reaching your goal or you could be waiting for a long time as life passes you by. Take charge and create those opportunities for yourself. What are you waiting for?

Yellow   You feel that there is so much you want and need to learn before you get a chance at your ideal life. Let's look at this from a different perspective. We never stop learning. Why is reaching your ideal life so different from the rest of the goals you have reached in your life. Make a plan for yourself. What do you feel you need to learn to prepare yourself for your new life? Now, as you go about acquiring this knowledge be aware that your new life does not have to wait until you are finished with this learning. Learning and living well are not mutually exclusive.

Green   You are waiting to be in better health or in better shape before you go for your new life. Again, you can do both simultaneously. This is not a matter of either / or. Develop a plan for getting healthier and at the same time establish the goal of your new life. You can work toward both together. Or, ask yourself if you are using your health as an excuse to not be happy. Maybe there is something deeper that you need to look into here.

Blue   You are having a difficult time saying good by to those people you feel will not be part of your new life. You are slowing down your own progress because you want to enjoy these friendships a little longer. My question would be "why do you feel these people can not be a part of your new life?" Is it because your new life will have new behaviors or habits or life styles? Why are you dreading leaving these people? Maybe what they offer is what you are looking for but do not realize it. Or, you are addicted to dreaming and making this new life a reality would leave you without a dream. You need to have some internal dialogue as to why you don't want to more forward just yet.

Purple   This is a color that I see often in the valley. The reason is that many spiritual people have the erroneous belief that they need to suffer. That they should not want for a better life because it is not spiritual to do so. If you believe that your spirituality has given you the ability to manifest, then you are wasting that effort. It is there for the asking, you just need to feel that you deserve it. Somewhere along the line you came to believe that spiritual means poor and mistreated. It's time to revisit your spiritual beliefs and see if you have misunderstood or made wrongful assumptions.

Mountain This area of the picture speaks to reaching your goals. The mountain speaks of strength, stability, and being eternal. I don't see as many color variations in this area. But those that I see make strong statements.

Green   Your long term commitment to yourself is to stay healthy and enjoy life to its fullest. You want to experience life, not just read about it or talk about it. You want to be active and outdoors. Your senses are hungry for life.

Purple   Your long term commitment to yourself is to stay grounded in strong spiritual beliefs. You want to be good. You want to help others. You want to live above the mundane. You don't want to worry about the survival level, but rather focus on the higher things.

Silver   You are looking forward to the good life. You want to have a wealthy and comfortable life style. You feel that money will make a difference in how much you enjoy life.

Brown   You feel that you will reach you ideal life but that it will take much discipline to stay there. You are already thinking about what routines you will have and how strict you will need to be with yourself and those around you.

Sun This area speaks of the guidance you feel you are getting from the universe, your guides, your counselors, or higher-self.

Red   You feel frustrated because you can't always hear that inner voice. You want more visible guidance in your life. You feel you have to figure too many things out by trial and error. Maybe a class in meditation or Yoga will help open up that inner voice a bit more. Or, maybe your spiritual source has a support group for you to join. You need to continue looking for this inner-voice, but in the meantime be aware that you haven't done that bad on your own. So don't despair.

Orange   You feel that your life is based on action/reaction. You are not convinced that there is anyone or anything guiding you.

Yellow   You feel that your intelligence and information is your guide. Logic will answer all of your questions. If you just apply your mind you will acquire what you look for.

Green   You feel that brute force is the way to get to where you need to get. You are very focused on the physical.

Blue   You feel that your guidance is provided by the people in your life. You want to make it there all together or not at all. You don't want to be alone and would rather have a lesser life with lots of friends than a fancier life alone.

Pink   Your guide all long has been love; your love for yourself and others. As long as you have love in your life everything else falls into place.

Purple   Your religion or spiritual beliefs are what guide you every step of the way.

Silver   You go where the money is. You feel you can buy anything and everything you want or need. So, your guide is money.

Blank   Leaving the sun blank means that you haven't given much thought to who or what guides you. You pretty much just do and know and don't worry about where it all comes from or where it all is leading to.

Candlelight

WORKING ON CLARITY, PURIFICATION, TRUTH

If you have chosen this diagram for your exercise then your inner-self is saying that you need to explore your higher consciousness. You are ready to move beyond the mundane and into a higher spiritual state.

The symbolism of this diagram is that each of us has a foundation from which to work from. And each one of us has a desire to explore higher truths and clarity around our life, its purpose, and it's direction.

Read through the below translation guide to explore what your drawing is expressing.

ONLY ONE COLOR ACROSS THE WHOLE PICTURE

This often indicates that you are having difficulties differentiating between what are basic life issues and spiritual issues. Everything is either good or bad to you. You allow one event or aspect of your life to dictate everything else in your life. If you have a bad morning, then the rest of your day will suffer. Similarly in relationships you tend to hold grudges and take a long time to forgive. Basically in this diagram it does not matter what the color is that is across the whole page, because this will change as your emotions change. What needs to change is how you allow one thing to take over everything. You need to learn to segment your life a little more. If your boss yells at you it is not your children's fault so why should it affect them? If your romantic relationship breaks up, why should this put you at odds with every other person in your life? Of course not all situations are this extreme.

If you have colored this picture all one color, then the suggested action deals with learning to have clearer boundaries between the various aspects of life: work, friends, family, and spiritual nature.

GENERAL SUGGESTED ACTION

This exercise is for making the statements that your life has multiple facets and each can function independently from the other. The path to a healthier, happier life is to balance the various aspects of life. Repeat the exercise following the pattern described here to make your picture.

Color the base of the candle with layers of pink, blue, and purple working from the bottom up. Have the colors touch each other but not overlap. Or, if you have difficulty not getting them to overlap, then leave a thin blank space between the colors. The flames of the candle should be colored with a blending of yellow, orange, and red. Keep repeating the exercise until you feel that you are peace with how the picture turns out. Keep this picture where you can look at it often. When you have an incident or event that puts you in a bad mood, take your picture out and look at it for a few minutes. Over the next few days you should start to notice how getting over these bad phases takes less and less time. Keep working on it until you feel you are no longer letting one event or situation overpower everything in your life.

SECTIONS AND COLORS

There are two main sections to this diagram. The base signifies the parts of yourself that make up your foundation. The three flames are the next main section to translate. These flames signify what truth you are seeking or what pure state you are trying to reach, and your path to enlightenment.

Base Often I see this section of the base multi-colored. So, when translating the base you should combine the translation from all the colors you used.

Blank	If you left the base blank, it means that you want to leave your past behind and just focus on your enlightenment. What has been has been and you don't want to dwell on the life you have already had; you want to focus on your ultimate goal.
Red	Red in the base means that you feel your strength of emotions have given you the right level of passion for life; these have gotten you to this point. You have worked on keeping your emotions clear and pure. You are not embarrassed or ashamed to show your emotions for they are a part of who you are.
Orange	You feel that before you could attain enlightenment you needed to prove that you could survive in the world. You take your ability to take care of the survival level as a right of passage. You are an action person and one to look for enlightenment in rituals and tests. You are not one to look for enlightenment by sitting on top of the mountain cross-legged for 20 years. You need to feel you are doing something to get there.
Yellow	You are a thinker. You want your enlightenment to make sense and be logical. You do not negate your spiritual self. But you are still trying to prove that it exists in logical terms. It is continual exercise for you to keep intellect and intuition in balance and working together to search for the truth.

Green   You believe that your body is a temple. That in order to attain spiritual purity and enlightenment you must have a pure and clean body. Clean living is a big part of your path to enlightenment.

Blue   Having the right support group is important to you. You believe in having a spiritual leader and spiritual brothers and sisters. The people aspect of your spiritual life is important to you. You believe that reaching enlightenment need not sacrifice your friendships.

Purple   Enlightenment is not just a goal in life, it is your calling in life. You are working toward becoming a spiritual leader.

Brown   You believe that the spiritual path requires discipline. You are strict with yourself because you need structure to be part of your path.

Black   The spiritual path still holds some mysteries for you. You are not sure what enlightenment is but you are willing to seek it.

Flames You might find it interesting that unlike the base, I usually see all three flames the same color. Maybe this is because many feel that seeking enlightenment is an all encompassing goal and it needs no further breakdown. However, if you have used a different color for each of the flames then it means that you have mapped out your road to enlightenment into steps, and these are the steps you are working on.

Blank   If you left all three flames blank, then you don't want to have a preconceived notion of what enlightenment is. Or, you do not feel worthy of defining what enlightenment will be. So, you want to approach this path toward enlightenment with a totally open mind and blank slate. If you only left one or two flames blank, your definition of enlightenment is very clear and narrow. You don't want to be distracted by going after too many things at once. Your focus is clear.

Red   To you, enlightenment will bring a passion for something that you feel lacking right now. You want to have a cause in your life and this is what enlightenment will bring for you.

Orange   Your enlightenment will hold a change in your life such as a new job or a change of residence. This change is major and brings a different level of survival.

Yellow   Your enlightenment will bring with it answers to many questions. Some seek enlightenment wanting peace. You, on the other hand, seek enlightenment because you have a thirst for knowledge.

Green   You want release from the pains and suffering of this physical body. You feel limited by your body. You are seeking for ways to accept your body and/or work around the limitations you feel exist.

Blue   Blue flames talk about wanting to unite with others. In many cases this means uniting with loved ones who have passed. You believe that enlightenment will bring with it the ability to see the spirits of loved ones.

Purple   Enlightenment is not just a goal in life but your calling in life. You are working toward becoming a spiritual leader. Enlightenment for you will mean being able to share the truths you have learned.

GENERAL SUGGESTED ACTION

Some people have found this exercise helpful for reaching a state of higher consciousness. The symbolism in this exercise is to open up a doorway for you to accelerate your path to enlightenment. Repeat the exercise but this time start with the larger flame. Select the color that appeals to you when you focus on the goal of enlightenment. Now color the larger flame but go beyond the boundaries to turn it into a flame that is the whole center of the candle. This flame should now go from the bottom of the base of the candle and all the way to the tip of the candle. If you feel the need to color the rest of the diagram go ahead. Make sure the main part of the picture is this huge flame that is now superimposed as the center of the diagram. The message back to your inner-self is that you want to draw from your foundation and open up a doorway into enlightenment. After you finish this exercise, sit in meditation for at least 15 minutes. This gives your inner-self some time to digest the message and start to act on it. Many people have told me that after going through this exercise they experience very meaningful dreams for days afterwards, be prepared to keep a dream log next to your bed.

Woman in Lotus Flower

BALANCING POWER, HEALTH, BEAUTY

If you have chosen this diagram for your exercise, it says that you are already in one form or another on the path to enlightenment. You are now working on the details and fine tuning your spiritual self. You are aware of what you need to do to connect with your higher self. What you are looking for is additional spiritual tools to work with.

Whether you are male or female does not make a difference in what choosing this diagram means. You are looking for balance between your inner-self and your external expression. You want to live in an enlightened state but you also want to live in this world. You tend to go between both states of consciousness, so keeping grounded is something you constantly work on.

ONLY ONE COLOR ACROSS THE WHOLE PICTURE

This diagram is a very interesting one when only one color is used. The reason is that usually I see the same color used but drawn in different shades, strokes, and strengths of the same color. This says that there is one aspect of yourself that you are feeling out of balance and are trying to get it back in balance with the rest of your energies. This may be a specific lesson you are working through. Or, it may mean that the challenges life has presented you are activating a particular aspect of yourself; meaning there are still buttons that can be pushed.

The color that you chose tells you what aspect is out of balance:

Red   You have encountered something that you feel is unjust or unfair; a "how can this happen?" type of situation. You need to take a step back and look beyond the emotions that this situation has awakened. There is a reason why this has happened and it is an opportunity for a lesson or for repaying of karma. Look at the situation from all angles but always with love and spiritual awareness as the objective. **Suggested Action** – give your body a way to express this pent up energy. Go for a walk, do some exercise, sing opera, or take a blank sheet of paper and fill it up with the strong bold strokes of red color. Now that this energy has been vented, sit in a relaxed position and close your eyes. Take a slow deep breath and hold it for a few counts then slowly exhale.

Repeat another two times. Breathing normally continue to sit in your relaxed position with your eyes closed. In your mind's eye, see yourself sitting and surrounded by a soft white cool mist. Feel it refresh and calm you. Feel it heal your pain. With each inhale breathe in this refreshing, healing white mist. With each exhale breathe out the remaining red energy. After a few breaths you will notice that the red you are exhaling is softer and softer until it is more of a pink color. Thank your inner-self for communicating and working with you to bring back a balanced state. Count to three and open your eyes. Take a deep breath. You are done with the exercise.

Blue

You feel that your calling to share your truths has gotten you into confusing situations with other people. You are finding rejection from others, or that others are not taking your information as seriously as you would like. Take a check-point. Are you trying to make your truth a universal truth? Have you crossed the line between enlightened and fanatical about your truth? Maybe it is not up to you to evangelize. Ask yourself how you would take it if someone was presenting something to you in the way you have been presenting to others. Maybe your approach needs some softening. Or, maybe you need to lead by example instead of words.

Purple

This color also speaks of having the need to "spread the word" overshadows other important aspects of your spiritual life. Remember that sometimes when we are in denial about something to correct in ourselves we tend to focus on other's problems and faults. So, take a break from working with others and focus on yourself for a while.

Sparkly

Having sparkles show up in this picture usually means that you are having a difficult time staying grounded. You need to take a nature walk. Or if this is too far for you to go, then go to a zoo, or a garden. You need to be in contact with nature as a way to get grounded. Hold a piece of wood, a rock, or flowers in your hand as a way to get back to a grounded state.

OVERALL SUGGESTED ACTION

You need to bring it back in balance by repeating the exercise and this time make an effort to use different colors. Work on having the colors be coordinated; this works on harmony. Try and use the same strength throughout the various colors; this works on balance. Work on making all this work together into a pretty picture; this works on your internal and external beauty. Take your favorite color and darken the outline of each detail of the picture; this works on strength and definition. Now take a golden color and lightly fill in the background of the picture; this works on tapping into the power of the universe.

SECTIONS AND COLORS

Before you start translating the colors, analyze the starting point of your picture. If you worked from the outside in, your spiritual focus is on receiving your strength and power from higher sources. If you started from the inside out, you are working on balancing your energies and finding your own power. If you colored the woman's Chakras first, you are more focused on developing your internal beauty. If you colored the woman's body first, you are more focused on developing your external beauty. To understand what aspects or energies you are working through to arrive at these personal goals combine the translations provided based on the colors you applied in each of the sections.

Lotus Petals The petals of the Lotus Flower signify the expression of your power and beauty. How you choose to express this power and what the source of the power are both expressed through the petals.

Blank	This sometimes means that you are not ready to show your power. You are still unsure or maybe even afraid of your own power. You are being cautious as to how fast and how much you progress in this path before showing your power.
Red	This indicates that your power tends to come across to people as strong emotion. You might not be aware that you are using emotions to express you power. This sometimes comes across as an aggressive nature or a turbulent personality. Even if what you are expressing is positive, it probably won't be taken as positive due to the delivery style. It is suggested that you work on softening your outward expression so that you have a better chance of being heard. It is almost as if you are yelling your power when all you need to do is whisper. **Suggested Action** -repeat the exercise and consciously add a balancing color to ensure that your power is coming from a positive place. The balancing color can be in the petals or in the center of the Lotus Flower.
Orange	You tend to express your power in your lifestyle. You like to have extravagant things; fancy cars and big houses. You know how to use your power for manifestation. You are generous and helpful. You are also a bit flamboyant. Those who don't know you believe that you are all about money and that without it you would be powerless. But those who do know you, know that there is much more depth to you than just the superficial expression.
Yellow	The way you express your power is through sharing of information. You enjoy teaching and impressing others with the things you know. You are thought of by others as very intelligent and knowledgeable in many areas.
Green	You express your balance through your physical body. You enjoy looking good and being physically fit. To you beauty, health, and power are all strongly inter-related. You work hard at being healthy, strong, and beautiful.

Blue	You enjoy showing your power by being the "Go To" person. You like people coming to you for help. You are a caretaker personality type. But, sometimes this can get out of balance and you start to encourage and almost enjoy dependent relationships. These dependent relationships drain your energy and may even put you into a downward spiral. **Suggested Action** - repeat the exercise and this time make sure that the blue is contained within the petals. If you feel like you are fighting yourself doing this, then take a green or gold color and trace over the outlines of the inner circle of the flower, the flame, and the woman's body. This sends a message to the inner-self that the setting of boundaries is done with spiritual health in mind.
Purple	Your power is totally based on your spiritual nature, beliefs, and dedication. This is an unending source. It is a source that requires continuous focus from you. Daily meditation, cleansing, and spiritual commitment will maintain this power strong and pure. When you can maintain all your petals a strong purple you are transcending to the point of being able to work miracles.
Gold	Your power is totally based on your spiritual nature, beliefs, and dedication. This is an unending source. The difference between this and purple is that gold indicates you are on a specific mission. You have a calling or a special spiritual duty that you are working on. Daily meditation, cleansing, and spiritual commitment will maintain this power strong and pure.

Center of Flower This section of the Lotus flower speaks of the filters that you put thoughts, actions, and expressions through before they make it to the outward realm. It is a bi-directional filter, so the same filter gets applied to what you hear, see, and experience.

Blank	It is common for me to see the center of the Lotus Flower remain blank. Often, this means that there is nothing interfering between the outer expression and the inner expression. This is a sign of spiritual honesty. Make sure to combine this translation with what is going on in the flame section. The two should be in synch with each other.
Red	To you, enlightenment brings passion for doing the right thing. Having the courage to look at the world and have an opinion on what is acceptable and what is not. The caution here is to remember that nothing is all one thing – all good or all bad. Take care to look at all sides before acting or taking a position. In other words, take care not to put the red out of balance by becoming fanatical about something.
Orange	The balance that you are accomplishing is starting to have an impact on your level of survival. This usually means that an adjustment to your career or type of work takes place. Or, and adjustment in your home life or place of residence. Sometimes the adjustment is not pleasant. But, keep in mind that it is a passage on to something better. You have asked your inner-self to bring

your beauty, health, and power into balance. the changes you experience are acting on this request.

Yellow   This indicates that you are balancing your intellect and intuition. It sometimes also indicates that you put your spiritual senses through a logic filter before sharing them with the world. You are spiritual, but you are very careful to come across as intelligent and grounded.

Blue   The work you are doing on yourself is focused on your own power, health, and beauty. However, there is a strong people aspect to your life and you always keep them in mind as you make decisions and plans. Taking them into consideration is a good balance. Take care not to go so far as to have these people control your power and decisions.

Purple   This indicates that your power is in your spiritual beliefs. It also acts as a filter. Everything you think, do, and express outwardly passes through this spiritual filter.

Flame around Woman The flame is the seat of your power. It is generated by you, even though it is sometimes augmented and recycled through external factors. It is important to see if you colored all the way up to the outline of the flame, stopped before, or went beyond. The size of the flame speaks to the amount of power as well as to your comfort level with it. Sometimes I see a powerful flame but it is very compact. This tells me the person is not yet comfortable with their power so they pull it in close and make it compact. Then there are people whose flame is not that strong in color but it extends outward to the point that it starts to get diffused – pushed beyond its normal limits. This tells me the person wants others to know who they are and how powerful they are. Often these same people assume they have more power than they really do. Also, these people tend to use their power frivolously because they are more interested in showing it off than applying it for a specific purpose. So, part of this exercise should be to check your flame's comfort zone.

Blank   This is of concern since you are saying you don't feel you have any power. You are severely out of balance here. You are probably very tired, confused, and frustrated. Feeling overwhelmed with your work and life. The good news is that everyone has power. So, in reality what is happening is that you just have not learned how to tap into your power. **Suggested Action** - take the picture you have drawn and add the color yellow or gold to your flame area. Make the flame as small or big as you feel comfortable with. This message back to your inner-self is that you want to learn how to acknowledge and tap into your power. Another suggestion is to repeat the picture with the colors you want it to have based on their meaning and then post it where you can see it every day. This will give your inner-self the blueprint of the balance you are working toward achieving.

Red	Your power is activated by emotion. If the emotions are positive, this is a good source of energy. However, if your power is activated by anger then you need to be careful because you will have a difficult time controlling it and eventually lose it. **Suggested Action** - repeat the exercise and consciously add a balancing color to ensure that your power is coming from a positive place. The balancing color can be in the petals or in the center of the Lotus Flower.
Orange	You are looking to connect your strength and power with your survival level. This may be good for starters and to get a feel for your level of energies. However, as you progress you need to decouple the two. Your strength and power should emanate from within you and be based on your higher wisdom. The color orange is tethering you to external energy. The risk in an orange power base is that if you lose your socio-economic position you lose your power base. The goal of finding your strength and power is so that it can sustain you through what ever life presents you with. **Suggested Action** -develop a plan to migrate your power base from an external energy to an internal energy. One way to do this is to repeat this color exercise. This time purposely add more yellow and gold to the orange. Follow the exercise at least once a week. Each time you repeat the exercise add more gold or yellow until the orange is more of a glow of the gold. This is sending a message to your inner-self that you are changing the frequency of your power base to a more positive, internal, and spiritual source.
Yellow	Your power is based on your knowledge and ability to process information. You probably have a natural ability for teaching, research, or creating inventions. When you are feeling drained or tired, reading or learning something new will actually re-energize you.
Green	You feel that your power is based on your physical strength and healthy constitution. Similar to the orange color, you are anchoring your power to something that is external and physical. The risk is that as the physical body ages or suffers ill health, your power dwindles accordingly. The objective is to have this power to sustain you through anything. Your power should not dwindle with age; on the contrary if age brings wisdom then you should be more powerful as you get older. Now, the exception is that often a weak body does affect the level of spiritual power. But it is not the illness that interferes with your power. What happens is that you spend all of your energy trying to heal the body and that energy is then no longer available for other things. There are specific exercises to correct this drain of energy but that is another set of exercises for another time. **Suggested Action** - I often see people making a correlation between their physical body and their power. An exercise that many have found helpful is that while working on the migration of the power source you actually enhance the physical connection. The reason

for this is that many people that make this physical body / power correlation do so because they need to feel they are safe and can defend themselves and loved ones from physical harm. You should not remove this feeling of safety without first replacing it. Repeat this exercise once a week. Each time connect the green in the petals all the way to the body of the woman. Consciously make the strokes bi-directional. Now, also with bi-directional strokes add gold and yellow to this flow of color. The message to the inner-self is that your power and health are interconnected and they strengthen and replenish each other. You are essentially generating and recycling energy to sustain your power. The other subliminal message here is that your physical safety comes from your spiritual power.

Blue

This speaks to balancing your inner power with the desire to help others. This too can be a sort of recycling of energy. As you help others you generate more energy for them and yourself. The difference here is that you don't want the blue crossing the boundaries of the flame. You especially don't want the blue traveling from the petals all the way to the body of the woman. The risk being that blue energy flow between the petals and the body are basing your power, health, and beauty on the opinions of others. In other words you may be powerful but you are giving the control of that power to others. This blue out of control is common in humanitarians and spiritual leaders because they have a difficulty saying "No" to people even if it means hurting themselves. **Suggested Action** - repeat the exercise and this time make sure that the blue is contained within the petals. If you feel like you are fighting yourself doing this, take a green or gold color and trace over the outlines of the inner circle of the flower, the flame, and the woman's body. This sends a message to the inner-self that the setting of boundaries is done with spiritual health in mind.

Purple

Your power is totally based on your spiritual nature, beliefs, and dedication. This is an unending source. It is a source that requires continuous focus from you. Daily meditation, cleansing, and spiritual commitment will maintain this power strong and pure. Keeping the flame strong in turn keeps health and beauty strong. It is a spiritual ecosystem.

Gold

Your power is totally based on your spiritual nature, beliefs, and dedication. This is an unending source. The difference between this and purple is that gold indicates you are on a specific mission. You have a calling or a special spiritual duty that you are working on. Daily meditation, cleansing, and spiritual commitment will maintain this power strong and pure. A golden flame means that you are in the doorway to other dimensions. It is just as important to know how to close this doorway as it is to learn how to keep it open. Control is a safety-valve. If you are walking around with this doorway open all the time, you can start to lose the distinction of what is of this dimension versus other dimensions.

Woman This section of the picture speaks to the balance between internal and external beauty. Ideally the Chakras and the body were colored in a coordinated manner. This would imply that a balance exists between the internal and external selves. If more emphasis was given to the body, currently you are more focused on the beauty aspect of yourself rather than your health or balance.

Blank	A blank body means that you feel that by focusing on other aspects of your balance the body will follow suit. Most likely you have colored in the Chakras and expect that by keeping them in balance your health and beauty will follow.
Red	The element that is interfering with your balance is anger, pain, and frustration. Your emotions are raw and active. They are getting in the way of you thinking straight. Follow the exercise and meditation to release red energy so that you can start to make progress on your balance. **Suggested Action** – give your body a way to express this pent up energy. Go for a walk, do some exercise, sing opera, or take a blank sheet of paper and fill it up with the strong bold strokes of red color. Now, that this energy has been vented, sit in a relaxed position and close your eyes. Take a slow deep breath and hold it for a few counts then slowly exhale. Repeat another two times. Breathing normally, continue sitting in a relaxed position with your eyes closed. Now in your mind's eye see yourself surrounded by a soft white cool mist. Feel it refresh and calm you. Feel it heal your pain. With each inhale breathe in this refreshing, healing white mist. With each exhale breathe out the remaining red energy. After a few breaths you will notice that the red you are exhaling is softer and softer until it is more of a pink color. Thank your inner-self for communicating and working with you to bring back a balanced state. Count to three and open your eyes. Take a deep breath. You are done with the exercise.
Orange	Your concerns of the survival level are getting in the way of you achieving a balanced state. **Suggested Action** - do the hammer and wall exercise so that you can obtain information on how to break through these concerns about work and home. Then come back and work on this exercise for balance. You might work the two pictures in parallel for a few weeks.
Yellow	Your intellect is working with you to obtain the balance you seek. You have learned new techniques and are putting them to work.
Green	You body is healing as you get more in balance. As you achieve balance, you will notice that you have more energy and stronger health
Blue	You are starting to be more at peace with yourself. You are not as self-conscious about who you are or what you look like. You are ready to tell the world "this is who I am, take it or leave it." You may still be influenced by what others say, but you are getting to feel more comfortable about yourself.

Purple You are working on becoming more psychic. You are fine tuning your body to be a channel for information from other dimensions or higher knowledge. A word of caution: you need to make sure you are learning how to control this state so that you are not walking around open all day and losing touch with your day-to-day life and responsibilities.

Woman's Chakras This section of the picture speaks to the balance between internal and external beauty. Ideally the Chakras and the body were colored in a coordinated manner. This would imply that a balance exists between the internal and external selves. If more emphasis was given to the Chakras, currently you are more focused on your internal self. Each Chakra has its own color that it resonates at. The guide below discusses what color each Chakra is supposed to have. If the color you have is not that color, you are out of balance and need to cleanse and re-energize that Chakra to its rightful color. Practicing the rainbow exercise below is one of the easiest ways to achieve Chakra balance.

Blank blank Chakras usually mean that you are not aware of how your energy centers work. You need to learn how Chakras work so that you can then work on getting them in balance. Follow the rainbow exercise described below

1st Chakra – root This Chakra resonates at a red frequency. It is raw and primitive energy. It is associated with basic instincts like physical survival, courage, sex, violence, and anger. If your 1st Chakra has any other color, you are out of balance as a result of the influence of the other color. Look to how the other colors are translated in previous sections to get an idea of what element is pushing you out of balance. Fore example, if you have orange in this Chakra then your anger stems from the problems you are having in the survival level; either at work or at home.

2nd Chakra – abdomen This Chakra resonates with an orange frequency. It is responsible for the survival level. Concerns with work, home, and stability are all processed through this Chakra. If the color is any other than orange, that element is putting you out of balance. For example, if dirty yellow is in this Chakra, it states that you have not been making smart decisions about your survival level. Getting help in getting spending under control or talking with a financial advisor may help get this back to an orange color.

3rd Chakra – solar plexus This Chakra resonates at a yellow frequency. This is a combination Chakra. It is the umbilical cord to our astral-self. It helps us deal in the real world while also allowing us to tap into our astral/inter-dimensional power source. When feeling tired, this is the Chakra to breathe through for a quick burst of energy. This is not a Chakra you ever want blocked because then you experience a sense of being lost, alone, and cut-off from the rest of the world.

4th Chakra – heart	This Chakra resonates at a green frequency. This is the love center. It channels compassion, love, patience, acceptance, and connects us to the rest of humanity. Because these energies are the foundation of spiritual balance, having this Chakra out of balance can greatly affect your health.
5th Chakra – throat	This Chakra resonates with a blue frequency. This is the center of expression; including writing, speaking, and art. This is a place that I tend to see a lot of color influence. For example, I tend to see many people with red in this Chakra which means that they tend to communicate from an emotional base instead of a truth or inter-personal perspective. I also sometimes see yellow influencing this center, meaning the person is too literal in their communications, probably having lots of relationships issues because of it.
6th Chakra – third eye	This Chakra resonates at a purple or indigo frequency. This is the clairvoyant center. I find this Chakra is blocked in many pictures. This means the person is not ready to embrace their intuition and this is putting them out of balance.
7th Chakra – crown	This Chakra resonates at a violet frequency. This is the connection to the higher-self and unity with the divine.

RAINBOW MEDITATION FOR CHAKRA BALANCING

Sit in a relaxed position and close your eyes. Take a slow deep breath and hold it for a few counts, then slowly exhale. Repeat another two times. Breathing normally, continue sitting in a relaxed position with your eyes closed. In your mind's eye see yourself sitting and surrounded by a soft white cool mist. Feel it refresh and calm you. Feel it heal you. With each inhale breathe in this refreshing, healing white mist. With each exhale breathe out the stress and concerns of the day. After a few breaths you will notice that you are calmer and in a deeply relaxed state.

Focus your attention on the 1st Chakra. Notice the color you see there and make a mental note for later, but don't analyze it right now. Right now, you just want to focus on cleansing and balancing this Chakra. Breathe in the white refreshing mist. When you exhale, exhale through the 1st Chakra. Exhale as if flushing the Chakra with white energy. From a visual perspective you can almost see a cascade of water gushing from behind the Chakra and pouring out in front of you as it takes all impurities with it. Now check the color of the Chakra. See it clear, shiny, and glowing red. It is almost pulsating with power. Now, as if turning a knob, imagine that you are fine tuning this flower shaped energy center. Turn it right and left until you feel that it is at a healthy level for you. You don't want to leave it too open or too closed, feel your correct power level for this Chakra.

Now, focus your attention on the 2nd Chakra. Notice the color you see there and make a mental note for later, but don't analyze it right now. Right now you just want to focus on cleansing and balancing this Chakra in your lower abdomen. Breathe in the white refreshing and energizing mist. When you exhale, exhale through the 2nd Chakra. Exhale as if flushing the Chakra with white energy. From a visual perspective you can see a cascade of water gushing from behind the spine, through the Chakra, and pouring out in front of you as it takes all impurities with it. Now check the color of the Chakra. See it clear, shiny, and glowing orange. It is humming with energy. Now, as if turning a knob, imagine that you are tuning this flower shaped energy center. Turn it right and left until you feel it is at a healthy level for you.

Continue this process with each of the remaining Chakras. First, flush white energy through the Chakra to cleanse it. Second, tune it to your proper strength by turning it right to close or left to open. Each Chakra will have its own correct setting. Not all Chakras will be same size. What you are currently dealing with in your life sets the requirements for the right balance between the Chakras.

When you have cleansed and tuned all 7 Chakras, visualize yourself with all of your Chakras superimposed. See your body surrounded by an egg shaped field of white energy. All in a neat package healthy, comfortable, and safe. Take a deep breath and hold it for a few counts, exhale slowly. Thank your inner-self for communicating and working with you to bring back a balanced state. Count to three and open your eyes. Take a deep breath. You are done with the exercise.

This balancing meditation should be done at least once a week. After you finish the exercise, you can make notes on the colors you saw and use the guides to translate them.

Man with Chakras

BALANCING HEALTH, STRENGTH, POWER

If you have chosen Man with Chakras as your coloring exercise, it says that you are working on the connection between body and mind. This exercise provides clues to go even a step further to the connection between body, mind, and spirit.

The symbolism of this diagram is that the internal aspect of ourselves is very much linked to what we portray outwardly and how we deal with the external world. Each of the flowers represents an energy center called by its Sanskrit name of "Chakra".

Each Chakra vibrates with its own signature in the form of energy frequency. When these energy centers are out of balance, the range of consequences can impact every aspect of your life. Each Chakra is related to a specific health area, emotion, and spiritual aspect. Consider that our body is one big energy field and each Chakra is a fuse. Now, imagine that one of the fuses is not working properly. The rest of the energy field tries to compensate for the bad fuse by taking energy from other areas. Then those drained areas start to become weak and so on. This is why keeping these Chakras clean and fine tuned is so important from a physical, mental, and spiritual perspective.

ONLY ONE COLOR ACROSS THE WHOLE PICTURE

This picture is focusing on you. One color across the whole picture means that this is your main concern about yourself. This may be what you are working on improving, or it may be identifying what area in you is out of balance.

The color that you chose tells you what aspect is out of balance:

Red   You are angry with yourself. You are frustrated because this body of yours is not doing what it is supposed to. You are blaming yourself for everything that is wrong in your life. You need to take a step back and approach yourself with less anger and more compassion. You need to work on self-love and self-acceptance.

Suggested Action – give your body a way to express this pent up energy. Go for a walk, do some exercise, sing opera, or take a blank sheet of paper and fill it up with the strong bold strokes of red color. Now that this energy has been vented, sit in a relaxed position and close your eyes. Take a slow deep breath and hold it for a few counts, then slowly exhale. Repeat another two times. Breathing normally continue sitting in a relaxed position with your eyes closed. In your mind's eye see yourself surrounded by a soft white cool mist. Feel it refresh and calm you. Feel it heal your pain. With each inhale breathe in this refreshing, healing white mist. With each exhale breathe out the remaining red energy. After a few breaths you will notice that the red you are exhaling is softer and softer until it is more of a pink color. Thank your inner-self for communicating and working with you to bring back a balanced state. Count to three and open your eyes. Take a deep breath. You are done with the exercise.

Blue   You are feeling socially awkward. You feel like you don't fit in and you want to fit in. If the color is a muddy blue, it says that the group you are trying to fit in with is not right for you; this is why you are feeling this awkwardness. If the color is a clear blue, then you are in a transition period. You may be moving from one socio-economic status to another and have not yet established your new circle of friends. You may be tempted to go back to the old group of friends. But, this color is saying to keep building the new one for it is the right one for you at this time in your life.

Green   Your main concerns are centered on your physical body and its health. You have as a goal to achieve a strong and healthy body. If the color is a muddy green, the feeling is that your health is not good. Your system needs cleansing and healing. If the color is a clear vibrant green, you are healthy and must then ask yourself why you are so focused on the physical body. **Suggested Action** – You need to think about your perceptions about yourself and give them a reality-check. If you feel you are not healthy, go to the doctor. If you have been to the doctor and you checked out fine, but you can't let go of the feeling of being sick then you need to meditate on what is causing you to feel this way. If you are in good health but the stress is that your body does not look the way you think it should then your meditation should focus on where these expectations came from and why. In addition to the meditation, you should also follow the below overall suggested action and go through that exercise every morning before starting your day until you feel your perceptions about your health and or body are back in balance with the rest of your life.

SECTIONS AND COLORS

Background This section of the picture speaks to what you feel is acting on you. In this section it is very important to analyze the strokes and shades. I have seen some pictures where the background colors are sharp with strokes that shoot toward the body. As you probably guessed, this indicates that the person is feeling attacked by their environment. So, if you filled in the background, take a look at how you filled it in. Did you color from the outside in toward the body? Then you are aware of the external influences in your life and you want to work on either protecting yourself from them or preparing to deal with them better. If you drew the color from the body out to the background, you are very aware of your influence on your environment. You are working on being a positive influence. Your concern for the environment and others is given equal importance to the concern you have about your self.

Blank	A blank background means that this is your time. You want to focus on your own balance, health, and strength before discussing the external aspects of your life. This does not mean you are in denial about the external influences. It simply means you have chosen your self as the starting point for bettering your life.
Red	Your inner-self is saying that you are living in an environment that is full of emotions; mostly negative emotions. The people around you, the place you work or live in are filled with anger, frustration, or pain and it is affecting you. Now, if the colors are traveling out from you to the background, then what is being said is that you are creating an environment of anger, frustration, or pain. So, take a close look at the direction that you drew the color. If it is going in both directions, then your environment and you are bringing out the worst in each other. You are feeding off each other's anger. There may need to be some external changes in addition to working on inner balance.
Orange	You are surrounded by people who are focused on the survival level. It appears that you are in an environment that measures people by their possessions and it is starting to push you out of balance. Again, there may be some external changes that need to take place in addition to working on your inner balance.
Yellow	You are surrounded by many intelligent people and lots of information. You are having trouble digesting all of this information. In other words, you may be having information overload. In addition, you are allowing these intelligent people to cause you to doubt yourself. Remember the converse is true if the color is going out from you.
Green	You are surrounded by people who are obsessed with their physical body and health. Like the orange, the people in your life are judging people by their appearance. This obsession on the physical body is throwing you out of balance.

Blue   The expectations and judgment of others is causing some of the imbalance you are feeling. You have given too much power to the people in your life and they are using this power against you. You need to reclaim control of your life. Start making decisions because they are right for you not because they are what is expected of you by others.

Purple   You are living in a spiritual environment. I see this when people are in monasteries, or spiritual retreats. The key is to make a note of the benefits of this influence so that you can duplicate the experience even when you are not in this physical location.

Man This section of the picture speaks to your image of yourself. Typically I see one color across the whole body and the Chakras then colored separately in different colors. With the body acting as more of a background to the Chakras. However, if I look closer, there is usually a variance in the shade of the color in some places. So, look closer at your picture. If the color is softer or weaker in some areas than in others, then your inner-self is pointing out to you that these parts of your body need attention. This can mean that your inner-self is detecting vulnerability in that part of the body. You should take action to strengthen that part of the body that your inner-self has identified through a weaker color.

Blank   A blank body says that you feel that by focusing on other aspects of your balance the body will follow suit. Most likely you have colored in the Chakras and expect that by keeping them in balance your health and strength will follow.

Red   The element that is interfering with your balance is anger, pain, and frustration. Your emotions are raw and active. They are getting in the way of you thinking straight. Follow the exercise and meditation to release red energy so that you can start to make progress on your balance. **Suggested Action** – give your body a way to express this pent up energy. Go for a walk, do some exercise, sing opera, or take a blank sheet of paper and fill it up with the strong bold strokes of red color. Now that this energy has been vented, sit in a relaxed position and close your eyes. Take a slow deep breath and hold it for a few counts, then slowly exhale. Repeat another two times. Breathing normally continue sitting in a relaxed position with your eyes closed. In your mind's eye see yourself sitting and surrounded by a soft white cool mist. Feel it refresh and calm you. Feel it heal your pain. With each inhale breathe in this refreshing, healing white mist. With each exhale breathe out the remaining red energy. After a few breaths you will notice that the red you are exhaling is softer and softer until it is more of a pink color. Thank your inner-self for communicating and working with you to bring back a balanced state. Count to three and open your eyes. Take a deep breath. You are done with the exercise.

Orange	Your concerns of the survival level are getting in the way of your achieving a balanced state. **Suggested Action** - do the hammer and wall exercise so that you can obtain information on how to break through these concerns about work and home. Then, come back and work on this exercise for balance. You might work the two pictures in parallel for a few weeks.
Yellow	Your intellect is working with you to achieve the balance you seek. You have learned new techniques and are putting them to work.
Green	You body is healing as you get more in balance. You notice that as you achieve balance, you have more energy and stronger health. This is a color where you especially want to look for the variance in shades as a clue to what part of your health to work on.
Blue	You are starting to be more at peace with yourself. You are not as self-conscious about who you are or what you look like. You are ready to tell the world "this is who I am, take it or leave it." You may still be influenced by what others say, but you are getting to feel more comfortable about yourself.
Purple	You are working on becoming more psychic. You are fine-tuning your body to be a channel for information from other dimensions and/or higher knowledge. A word of caution: you need to make sure you are learning how to control this state so that you are not walking around open all day and losing touch with your day-to-day life and responsibilities.

GENERAL SUGGESTED ACTION

If your inner-self is telling you that you are not comfortable with whom you are then this exercise is a good one to follow. Often what is out of balance is our self-image. Lack of self-confidence and self-love is more harmful to us than almost anything the world can throw at us. So, this exercise helps to enhance self-confidence and self-love. Repeat the exercise, this time take a gold or purple color and trace the outline of the body. This creates a protective shield around you so that you can better function in an unfriendly environment. Now, color the body area a nice pink. Select a pink that you feel comfortable with. When you look at this pink, there should be some sort of reaction in you. Sometimes, I hear people say that their heart did a little jump, or there is a feeling of warmth in the chest or arms. These reactions are your body asking to be fed this color. Use this pink color on the body section of the picture. This is sending a message to the inner-self as well as the conscious self to love who you are, even if you are not perfect. That you are working to achieve a better state, and you love yourself and accept yourself at every stage of the journey. Now, color the Chakras according to their proper color as described below. Work at this picture until you feel happy and warm when you see it. You can even have sparkles and a golden glow in the background to enhance the image. Keep this picture where you can see it often so that the blueprint you have designed is transmitted to the subconscious as its new working orders.

Man's Chakras This section of the picture speaks to the balance between the internal and external self. Ideally, the Chakras and the body were colored in a coordinated manner. This would imply that a balance exists between the internal and external selves. If more emphasis was given to the Chakras, currently you are more focused on your internal self. Each Chakra has its own color frequency that it resonates at. The guide below discusses what color each Chakra is supposed to have. If the color you have is not that color, then you are out balance and need to cleanse and re-energize that Chakra to its rightful color. Doing the rainbow exercise below is one of the easiest ways to achieve Chakra balance.

Blank	blank Chakras usually mean that you are not aware of how your energy centers work. You need to learn how Chakras work so that you can then work on getting them in balance. Follow the rainbow exercise described below.
1st Chakra – root	This Chakra resonates at a red frequency. It is raw and primitive energy. It is associated with basic instincts like physical survival, courage, sex, violence, and anger. If your 1st Chakra has any other color, you are out of balance as a result of the influence of the other color. Look to how the other colors are translated in previous sections to get an idea of what element is pushing you out of balance. Fore example, if you have orange in this Chakra then your anger stems from the problems you are having in the survival level; either at work or at home.
2nd Chakra – abdomen	This Chakra resonates with an orange frequency. It is responsible for the survival level. Concerns with work, home, and stability are all processed through this Chakra. If the color is any other than orange, that element is putting you out of balance. For example, if dirty yellow is in this Chakra, it states that you have not been making smart decisions about your survival level. Getting help in getting spending under control or talking with a financial advisor may help get this back to an orange color.
3rd Chakra – solar plexus	This Chakra resonates at a yellow frequency. This is a combination Chakra. It is the umbilical cord to our astral-self. It helps us deal in the real world while also allowing us to tap into our astral/inter-dimensional power source. When feeling tired, this is the Chakra to breathe through for a quick burst of energy. This is not a Chakra you ever want blocked because then you experience a sense of being lost, alone, and cut-off from the rest of the world.
4th Chakra – heart	This Chakra resonates at a green frequency. This is the love center. It channels compassion, love, patience, acceptance, and connects us to the rest of humanity. Because these energies are the foundation of spiritual balance, having this Chakra out of balance can greatly affect

your health.

5th Chakra – throat	This Chakra resonates with a blue frequency. This is the center of expression; including writing, speaking, and art. This is a place that I tend to see a lot of color influence. For example, I tend to see many people with red in this Chakra which means that they tend to communicate from an emotional base instead of a truth or inter-personal perspective. I also sometimes see yellow influencing this center, meaning the person is too literal in their communications, probably having lots of relationships issues because of it.

5th Chakra – throat : This Chakra resonates with a blue frequency. This is the center of expression; including writing, speaking, and art. This is a place that I tend to see a lot of color influence. For example, I tend to see many people with red in this Chakra which means that they tend to communicate from an emotional base instead of a truth or inter-personal perspective. I also sometimes see yellow influencing this center, meaning the person is too literal in their communications, probably having lots of relationships issues because of it.

6th Chakra – third eye : This Chakra resonates at a purple or indigo frequency. This is the clairvoyant center. I find this Chakra is blocked in many pictures. This means the person is not ready to embrace their intuition and this is putting them out of balance.

7th Chakra – crown : This Chakra resonates at a violet frequency. This is the connection to the higher-self and unity with the divine.

RAINBOW MEDITATION FOR CHAKRA BALANCING

Sit in a relaxed position and close your eyes. Take a slow deep breath and hold it for a few counts, then slowly exhale. Repeat another two times. Breathing normally, continue sitting in a relaxed position with your eyes closed. In your mind's eye see yourself sitting and surrounded by a soft white cool mist. Feel it refresh and calm you. Feel it heal you. With each inhale breathe in this refreshing, healing white mist. With each exhale breathe out the stress and concerns of the day. After a few breaths you will notice that you are calmer and in a deeply relaxed state.

Focus your attention on the 1st Chakra. Notice the color you see there and make a mental note for later, but don't analyze it right now. Right now, you just want to focus on cleansing and balancing this Chakra. Breathe in the white refreshing mist. When you exhale, exhale through the 1st Chakra. Exhale as if flushing the Chakra with white energy. From a visual perspective you can almost see a cascade of water gushing from behind the Chakra and pouring out in front of you as it takes all impurities with it. Now check the color of the Chakra. See it clear, shiny, and glowing red. It is almost pulsating with power. Now, as if turning a knob, imagine that you are fine tuning this flower shaped energy center. Turn it right and left until you feel that it is at a healthy level for you. You don't want to leave it too open or too closed, feel your correct power level for this Chakra.

Now, focus your attention on the 2nd Chakra. Notice the color you see there and make a mental note for later, but don't analyze it right now. Right now you just want to focus on cleansing and balancing this Chakra in your lower abdomen. Breathe in the white refreshing and energizing mist. When you exhale, exhale through the 2nd Chakra. Exhale as if flushing the Chakra with white energy. From a visual perspective you can see a cascade of water gushing from behind the spine, through the Chakra, and pouring out in front of you as it takes all impurities with it. Now check the color of the Chakra. See it clear, shiny, and glowing orange. It is humming with energy. Now, as if turning a knob, imagine that you are tuning this flower shaped energy center. Turn it right and left until you feel it is at a healthy level for you.

Continue this process with each of the remaining Chakras. First, flush white energy through the Chakra to cleanse it. Second, tune it to your proper strength by turning it right to close or left to open. Each Chakra will have its own correct setting. Not all Chakras will be same size. What you are currently dealing with in your life sets the requirements for the right balance between the Chakras.

When you have cleansed and tuned all 7 Chakras, visualize yourself with all of your Chakras superimposed. See your body surrounded by an egg shaped field of white energy. All in a neat package healthy, comfortable, and safe. Take a deep breath and hold it for a few counts, exhale slowly. Thank your inner-self for communicating and working with you to bring back a balanced state. Count to three and open your eyes. Take a deep breath. You are done with the exercise.

This balancing meditation should be done at least once a week. After you finish the exercise, you can make notes on the colors you saw and use the guides to translate them.

Eternal Flame within Lotus Flower

FINDING THE ETERNAL SELF

If you have chosen the Eternal Flame as your coloring exercise, this in itself gives a clue. The clue is that you are feeling the need to find your life's purpose. You are seeking answers to what there is beyond this life. You are ready to embark on the journey in search of these answers.

There are two key symbols in this diagram. The first symbol is the Lotus Flower, which signifies the universe. The second symbol is the flame, which signifies your own eternal essence. Some people have even found the meaning of this combination of images to mean their own essence as it travels through the wheel of life in search of perfection.

STARTING POINT

Where did you begin coloring? As in other diagrams, the starting point provides clues to where your journey should begin, or where you currently are in your journey.

LOTUS PETALS

Starting at the petals says that you have information in your past lives that will help you in your search for answers. If you colored the petals as overlapping, you want to focus on the details of your past lives; questions like who were you? What did you accomplish? Where did you live?

If you colored the overlapping areas differently from the rest of the petals, this says that you are more interested in finding out about the in-between state. You want to know what happens when we die. You are not as interested in past lives; you just want to know about the "other side".

CENTER OF THE LOTUS

Starting at the center says you are in search of a belief system that will bring you answers. Perhaps you are transitioning from one belief system to another. What you do know is that you are not sure about what you believe in, although you know there is something to believe in, and so you search.

FLAME

Starting with the flame says that your focus is on your higher-self; your astral-self. You are aware of the other aspects of the diagram but they are not as urgent to explore as your higher-self. So, your questions are not "what is in the universe?" but rather "where do I fit in?" "Who am I, and what is my role in the scheme of things?"

ONLY ONE COLOR ACROSS THE WHOLE PICTURE

This is one of the few diagrams that I have never found a single color picture. I see some with just a few colors and some with almost every color in the spectrum, but I don't remember ever seeing one with just one color.

I have come across people that resist coloring this diagram and they leave it blank. In most of those cases the situation was that they were not ready to tackle the idea of eternity. Or they were not ready to even discuss things beyond themselves. These were clients who had some very serious issues going on in their survival level and the sense of urgency they felt toward these issues made them not want to focus on anything other than the immediate situation.

SECTIONS AND COLORS

Typically I see two types of pictures with this diagram. One type is where the picture is a blending of related colors – purple, violet, pink. The other type is where I see every color in the spectrum. Each style tells a story. It should be noted that I have seen the same person create both types of pictures, depending on what they were working on

The blending of related colors says that you have found that everything in our life is inter-related. When something is right or something is wrong there is s domino effect; nothing happens in a vacuum. The key here is that the colors you are blending are the areas of your life that are coming into harmony to bring forth answers. The translation needs to take this into consideration. Combine the color translations in a manner that they are progressing from one to the other. So, instead of separate thoughts, they should instead flow together as if they are sentences in the same paragraph.

The style where many colors are used speaks about a person that wants to make sense of everything in their life all at once. They feel they have learned so much, experienced so much, it all must have a meaning. This is a good acknowledgement of your life. To come to the realization that everything you have ever done, experienced, planned, failed at, succeeded at, everything is part of the picture. This in itself starts to move a step closer toward seeing the purpose of this life. It is a feeling of having all the pieces to the puzzle on the table, and some of them have even been put together. But, like a puzzle, there is a strategy for how to approach the creation of the picture. So, the lesson is, yes you have taken inventory that all the pieces are there. Now, take a step back and choose one or two places to start; it will make the process go faster and easier.

Lotus Petals The petals of the Lotus Flower speak of your life times. The color of the petal speaks to the aspect of that life that is acting on your present journey.

Blank	You want to focus on what this lifetime is doing and how to use this information in your search for answers.
Red	This is a lifetime that has many lessons on emotions. It was probably a difficult life with much anger and pain. The fact that it has shown up means that there is a situation in your life right now that is trying to bring closure to the karma associated with the pain and anger from that past life.
Orange	This is a life time where making ends meet was a constant challenge. It may be a life where you were very poor. Or it may be a life where you went from being wealthy to losing everything. There are some fears for the survival level that connect back to this life time; and they need to be resolved. The lessons in an orange life are responsibility, stability, and survival. One place to start working on closure for this orange life is using an exercise that deals with these elements; like the sunrise/sunset diagram.
Yellow	This was a life where your information, knowledge, and intelligence were the theme of your life. Maybe you were a teacher, inventor, or scientist. Sometimes, a yellow life is where you made some discoveries and found some truths. By focusing on the yellow life you may bring forth memories of what these truths were and apply them in today's life.
Green	This was a life where you worked as a healer or in the health field. When these lives show up with strong strokes they usually speak of a connection to your present attitude toward health. So, if you are currently very obsessed with your health or physical condition you might be responding to memories from that life time. For example, someone who died of starvation in one life time may become obese in another. Or, someone who was physically abused in one lifetime may need to feel safe in this life by always working on body strength.
Blue	This was a life where the theme was people. Blue life times have as their lessons friendship, loyalty, and self-sacrifice for the greater good.
Purple	This was a life where you were a spiritual leader. The theme and lessons were regarding belief systems, faith, spirituality, and personal growth.

Center of Flower The center of the flower speaks to your journey in search of information and answers. This is your connection to universal truth.

Blank	This means that you have not learned how to connect to the realm of higher knowledge. If you have color in the petals and color in the flame, then a blank center means that you have all of the pieces but haven't figured out how they fit together yet.
Red	It is your passion for the truth that will enable you to find answers.
Orange	It is your ability to turn something esoteric into practical application that will allow you to find your answers.
Yellow	It is your dedication to knowledge and learning that will bring you to the answers you seek.
Blue	For you, working with a group is the way that you will find your truth. You need the validation of a support group to help you on this journey.

Flame This flame represents your spiritual-self. Your wisdom and knowledge feed this flame. Before looking at the colors, analyze the size of the flame. Did you color all the way to the boundaries of the flame? Did you extend beyond the outline of the flame? Or, did you leave some blank space between your color and the flame outline? The size of the flame speaks of how confident you are in your spiritual-self. If your flame is small, it says that you are feeling that you are just starting out on this path. You are almost shy about admitting to yourself that you are a spiritual being. A large flame that extends beyond the outline says that you are very confident in your spiritual knowledge and truth. In this case there might be something else on this picture that you are working on, since it appears that your spiritual confidence does not need help. If the color goes right up to the outline but does not go beyond the flame it says that you feel you are at the right place and time to venture forth on your journey. You feel ready and able.

Blank	I don't see this very often. The times that I have, the person was feeling very defeated. They felt they had tried so hard and gotten nowhere. They were tired and drained. So, a blank flame may mean that you need to rest and reenergize before going forward. Be assured that this is a temporary setback. **Suggested Action** - fill in the flame with a golden color. This tells your inner-self to tap into higher energy to refuel your power center. Now, wait a day or two and repeat the exercise to see if you are back.
Red	You are very anxious to get started; almost too much so. You are passionate about your search. You need to release some of the excitement and emotion before proceeding. You are vibrating at too strong a frequency to be a clear receptor. **Suggested Action** - add some white to the color so that it becomes more of a pink color. Focus on that color until you feel yourself getting calmer. Then, continue with the translation, or do the exercise again.

Orange

You are an action person and you feel that you have been doing too much thinking and planning and not enough "doing". Similar to the red, you need to release some of this physical energy before proceeding on your journey, because it is interfering with your reception. Prior to meditating, you should go for a walk, stretch, or do something physical to release this energy. **Suggested Action** - add some yellow to the flame so that your color becomes more of a gold hue. This lets your inner-self know that you can detach enough physically to be able to focus spiritually.

Yellow

You are intellectualizing too much. You have a case of spiritual analysis paralysis. You are a thinker by nature so this is something you will need to work on consciously. Make an effort to put the analysis off to the end. Allow yourself to receive information, document it, and then take the time to analyze it. Right now you are trying to do both at the same time and working against yourself.

Green

Your inner-self considers your body a temple. Therefore, for you, the path to enlightenment is through a clean and pure body.

Blue

It is your love for people that will give you the insight to the truth you are seeking. By observing others in their search for truth you will be able to see what your own journey will hold.

ABOUT THE AUTHOR

Martha Soria Sears is a clinical hypnotherapist and a business and personal transformation consultant. For thirty years she has given classes and coached people on how to bring about change in their lives. Her clients are from all walks of life. Martha uses a multi-disciplinary approach in her transformation consulting that includes working with the five senses, color, visualization, and hypnotherapy. Her unique approach has been proven successful both in a business setting as well as in personal day-to-day applications.

Early on in her work Martha noticed that talking with people and providing information was not enough to bring about change in their situation. Her clients felt they needed to own their solution in a more tangible way. Martha responded to this need by developing tools and techniques that allowed her clients to participate in the solution design by allowing their inner-self to provide input and feedback throughout the process.

Martha is the founder and president of SorSea, a company dedicated to the development of self-help products, tools, workshops, and books. Martha and her family currently live in Beaverton, Oregon.